OPENING TO GOD

OPENING TO GOD

*Guided Imagery Meditation on Scripture
for Individuals and Groups*

❧

CAROLYN STAHL

THE UPPER ROOM

OPENING TO GOD

Scripture quotations in this publication are from *The New English Bible,* © The Delegates of the Oxford University Press and the Syndics of the Cambridge University Press 1961 and 1970, and are reprinted by permission.

Library of Congress Catalog Card Number: 77-87403

UR-357-20-5-1283

Thank You

to the many people who have participated in guided imagery.meditation on scripture, teaching me its effectiveness.

to Roger Johnson, who offered ideas, support, and feedback, both as I led meditations and as we listened to the tapes.

to Anne Schurman, who typed the original meditations with patience.

to Barry Woodbridge, who nudged me toward seeking publication, offered support, and made perceptive comments.

to the people who read the manuscript and gave suggestions: the "Burning Bush" interns at the School of Theology at Claremont (Theresa Mason, Chuck Cooper, Mitzi Eilts, Becky Beyer, Sharon Rhodes, Russ Locke, Jerry Allen, Cornelius Gray, Dennis Williams, Fran Cooper, and Mark Luera-Whitmore), Ben and Lysbeth Stahl, Annie Head, Barbara Rosenow, Naomi Guinn, and Roger Betsworth.

to Maxie Dunnam and Janice Grana, two compassionate editors.

to David Griffin, who made suggestions for significant changes.

to George Thompson, who read and reread with a keen eye to every detail.

to John Biersdorf, a seeker of the spirit, who graciously gave insight and the foreword.

to you, the reader, who are soon to begin an adventure.

to the dandelion, and its Creator.

CONTENTS

FOREWORD

RECENTLY I ATTENDED WORSHIP IN a large stone church in which the atmosphere of the liturgy and the sermon was not incongruent with the dull, cold, gray rock walls surrounding the congregation. The wall behind the altar, however, was in vivid color. Saints were painted on it in an ancient art form in which the head of each person was surrounded by a golden circle. The golden circles, halos, or auras, of course, were an old artistic convention, designed to suggest the saints' transforming experience of the presence of God. There was no indication that my fellow worshipers identified themselves in any way with the figures behind the altar, or that the experiences of God common to those early worshipers called *saints* might also be available that day to us in the church.

We are currently undergoing a cultural change of yet unknown, but probably enormous significance. It has to do with the realization that if we are to survive on this planet we must change our fundamental ways of being and doing. Specifically, we must balance our extraverted, competitive activism with a deeper wisdom, grounded in the experience of the presence of God, and issuing in sacramental action. Carolyn Stahl calls it the news within, and indeed it is news for many people, and not necessarily good tidings at that.

What we need are pioneers with the quiet courage to explore the inner places of deeper wisdom and to report their findings to us. We need people not just to tell us what they have learned, but also to enable us to find our own, more profound experience of God and wholeness. Ms. Stahl is clearly one such person. I am delighted with this book because it is so obviously based on

9

experience—her own personal search, and her experience in teaching others. Above all, it helps us to find those inner places for ourselves and so to become fellow journeyers in the exploration of inner space.

JOHN E. BIERSDORF

PREFACE

WHILE I WAS IN SEMINARY, I did not read a newspaper daily. Since I had decided that I wanted to push through school as quickly as possible, I eliminated many things from my schedule and budget, including the news. My values have changed over the past few years. Now I can hardly imagine not knowing what is going on in the world. If I ever become that busy again, I doubt that the news will be left by the wayside. Reading the news guarantees neither that I will be a responsible world citizen nor that I will be adequately informed. However, I have very little potential for being informed or responsible if I do not pay attention to the news.

In the past few years, my values have changed in another dramatic way. I have come to realize that I was not paying regular attention to the "news" being given from within. As I began to become aware of and to write down my dreams, for example, I saw how important "inner news" is to becoming a responsible world citizen. Reading the news is no guarantee for correct information or responsible action. Similarly, attending to inward information provides no guarantee that I will grasp the messages accurately. Neither does it guarantee that I will act wisely or responsibly on the basis of those messages. I have very little potential, however, for being responsible to my body-mind or to my friends and fellow-beings if I ignore the "news" from within.

The value of attention to the depths within has been underscored for me as I have been exploring meditation, journal keeping, dream understanding, prayer, and guided imagery. I became aware of this value especially during 1975-76 under the

Lilly Endowment funded "Project Burning Bush" at the School of Theology at Claremont, California. I have developed two overriding professional passions: to help Christian, church-related people to come alive to their spiritual journeys and to address the spiritual needs of people who are following paths which are not directly related to the Christian church.

The purpose of this book is to provide ideas and assistance for guided imagery meditation on scripture. This is one experiential approach for attending to the depths of the self and God.

PART ONE

❦

BACKGROUND
FOR
GUIDED IMAGERY
MEDITATION
ON
SCRIPTURE

CHAPTER ONE

IMAGERY MEDITATION

BACKGROUND INFORMATION

R EADING THE BIBLE HAS BEEN valuable as a devotional guide for many people throughout the years. However, the approach to meditation described in this book does not consist strictly of reading passages from the Bible. Rather, an individual will choose a biblical passage with concrete symbolism and then use the content and symbols of the passage as a loose structure, allowing his/her psyche to bring forth what it will. In this way, the biblical passage is used as a window frame through which one's depths, with Divine guidance, provide the scene.

Methods for bringing forth the symbolic potential of the psyche have been developed in many cultures. Ancient Greece and Egypt, India and China, and early Christianity all had ways of evoking a dream in order to seek guidance for practical use.[1] Francis Galton and Alfred Benet, modern psychologists in the late nineteenth and early twentieth centuries, were early pioneers in using mental imagery. Carl Happich, a German doctor, developed the method of suggesting predetermined scenes such as a meadow, a mountain, or a chapel to initiate imagery sessions in his work with clients. Martha Crampton, a Psychosynthesis therapist, describes Happich's perspective: "His emphasis was strongly religious and Christian, and his goal was spiritual integration."[2]

Jung made a valuable contribution in this area. He perceived that *active imagination* is something in which one could participate alone, not exclusively with an analyst. However, he would often reflect upon the client's imagery material as part of the analysis process later.[3] Jungian, Gestalt, and Psychosynthesis therapists, as well as many other growth-facilitators, use forms of imagery as one among many techniques to tap the resources of the psyche for guidance and richness of experience.[4]

Similarly, imagery meditation is being used by medical doctors to aid the human body's immunity system to fight off diseases, such as cancer. Dr. Carl Simonton is an example of a pioneer in this field.[5] If imagery meditation is used in doctors' offices (admittedly few thus far), counselors' offices, and growth groups, why not also use it in another setting which strives toward wholeness—the church? Through my experience with the use of imagery meditation in worship settings, small groups, and by individuals, I am convinced that it is a viable option.

In fact, this type of meditation is not new. It was being used in the church four hundred years ago. Saint Ignatius taught guided imagery based on biblical passages. He chose passages such as the Incarnation, Jesus at the Temple, the Last Supper, the Passion, and the Resurrection for such "mental image" meditations. The following is St. Ignatius's contemplation upon the Nativity. I have quoted it in its entirety to show the way in which St. Ignatius set the stage.

The first prelude is to review the history of the Nativity. How our Lady, almost nine months with child, set out from Nazareth, seated on an ass, as may piously be believed, together with Joseph and a servant girl leading an ox. They are going to Bethlehem to pay the tribute that Caesar has imposed on the whole land.

The second prelude is to form a mental image of the scene and see in my imagination the road from Nazareth to Bethlehem. I will consider its length and breadth, and whether it is level or winding through valleys and over hills. I will also behold the place of the cave of the Nativity, whether it is large or small, whether high or low, and what it contains.

The third prelude will be the same and in the same form as it was in the preceding contemplation.

The first point is to see the persons: our Lady and St. Joseph, the servant girl, and the Child Jesus after his birth. I will become a poor, miserable, and unworthy slave looking upon them, contemplating them, and ministering to their needs, as though I were present there. I will then reflect within myself in order that I may derive some fruit.

The second point is to observe, consider, and contemplate what they are saying and to reflect within myself that I may derive some profit.

The third point is to observe and consider what they are doing: the journey and suffering which they undergo in order that our Lord might be born in extreme poverty, and after so many labors; after hunger and thirst, heat and cold, insults and injuries. He might die on the cross, and all this for me. I will then reflect in order to gain some spiritual profit.

The Colloquy. Conclude with a colloquy as in the preceding contemplation and with the "Our Father."[6]

St. Ignatius suggested moving into the biblical episode, being there, listening, watching, and even conversing with the people within the scene. Because he repeated the instructions to reflect "within myself," it is clear he was not expecting the imagination exercise to be solely for understanding the biblical situation and teachings. He was expecting personal growth, too. Likewise, personal growth and understanding of the Bible are expected results of the techniques and meditations included in this volume.

There are some differences between his approach and the one taken in this book. I suggest that, when engaging in dialogue with people in the biblical scene, one can choose whether to let them into one's setting in time or to enter into their setting in time. Similarly, one can either stay close to the biblical meaning or let emerge through oneself whatever meanings come forth now. Where Ignatius was bold in getting across his theology within the meditation, I have attempted to allow maximum flexibility for the emergence of the individual's own divinely guided intuition and beliefs. I realize, though, that my theology *does* influence the structure of these meditations, even while I try to make them open-ended.

There are a number of books already published which explain

visualization and dream interpretation. Please see Suggested
Readings on pages 123–125.

SETTING THE STAGE: TWO MODES OF CONSCIOUSNESS

Biofeedback, parapsychology, and meditation research have
helped bring greater attention to the two modes of consciousness which are experienced by all persons and cultures. One
mode is predominantly analytic, logical, verbal, and linear in
function. In this mode, persons see the world as separate discrete objects and are concerned for biological survival. This
consciousness is identified with the left hemisphere of the brain,
the right side of the body, and often with the masculine and with
light. The other mode is one of intuition, art, and body movement in space. In this mode, things are viewed holistically and
relationally, rather than as separate discrete objects. This mode
is identified with the right hemisphere of the brain, the left side
of the body, and often with the feminine and with darkness and
mystery.[7]

It is not too difficult to observe that our culture has identified
with and overvalued the first mode of consciousness. Consequently, we have sadly limited our potential health, wholeness, creativity, and ability to relate. Attention to meditation,
body movement, art forms, dreams, intuition, and imagination
allows for greater emergence of the second mode of consciousness which is within us all.

I find that we Christians have especially limited our prayer
life to the verbal, separate, discrete-object mode. We have access
to Divine guidance through intuition, creativity, and a sense of
unity with all things, but most of us have not been using these
resources. Many of us have expressed our concerns to God in
prayer. However, we have neglected to still ourselves, to open to
God, and to listen. Both prayer *and* meditation, verbal *and*
intuitive-imaginative approaches offer potential for spiritual
growth.

Spiritual growth, as I am defining it, means openness to God
and the development and balancing of aspects of the body-mind.

The mind includes functions such as reason, will, intuition, imagination, and emotions. Thus we are growing spiritually as we seek to be open to God in developing functions such as imagination or reason and in balancing and integrating the various functions. The aim is attention to all of our functions. For example, as we develop flexibility of the body through exercise and mental flexibility through imagination exercises, both of these types of flexibility may carry over to our analytical "thinking." We will then become more flexible as we work on a problem, be it a scientific exploration or simply planning a budget. Body, imagination, and reason can work together to express God's aims through each of us.

TYPES OF MEDITATION AND THEIR PURPOSES

Several different types of meditation have been used in religious traditions for years. Most people immediately think of Eastern religions when they hear the word *meditation.* However, most types of meditation have been explored and used both in Eastern and Western religions . . . because they work.

Authors classify meditations in various ways. One of the most helpful classifications which I have studied is given by Robert E. Ornstein in *On the Psychology of Meditation* and in *The Psychology of Consciousness.* [8] Ornstein categorizes meditation into two types: *concentrative* and *opening-up.* In *concentrative* meditation, one seeks to let go of the chatter of thought which constantly occurs in the mind by focusing intensely and exclusively upon an object: sound (word, chant, sound in nature), prayer (long or short), physical movements (repetitive dance, routine gestures), visual object (symbol, picture, mandala, small round object), body function (heartbeat, breath), or combinations of these objects used simultaneously. After a period of such intense concentration, one is more alert to and aware of the fullness of life. One has practiced letting go of distractions, and the ability to focus attention or to concentrate is strengthened. Through this practice, a person can develop the ability to give greater attention to a friend in a conversation, a musical record, a book, a problem to be solved, or even to God.

In *opening-up* meditation, one seeks to be fully aware while one participates in action. One might do the dishes, fully attentive just to doing the dishes, not wandering in thought. Or one might "just sit," alert and not distracted by external or internal awareness. Archery and other forms of movement-martial arts are *opening-up*. Many meditations are combinations of these two types.

The meditations in this book are a "combination" of types. They are *concentrative* in that one lets go of other thoughts and focuses exclusively and intensively upon the scene that is given. They are also *opening-up* in that they include an alertness to the inner spontaneous flow of images, thoughts, and feelings. Consider the analogy of the window frame. The frame, the given biblical passage, is the *concentrative* element. The scene, the image, is the *opening-up* element in the meditation.

There are two additional purposes for these guided imagery meditations on scripture. One is to become aware where you are now. The other is to aim more precisely toward what seems to be a healthy, positive, and constructive direction. For example, you may be asked to visualize yourself in a grassy area. How you create that grassy area is a function of where you are at that time. You may then be asked to visualize the sun shining. That suggestion is for the purpose of aiming you constructively toward light, wisdom, God. . . . If you had imagined rain in your scene before you heard (or read) about the sunshine, you can simply acknowledge that rain is what you created first, then change it to sunshine. Or, if you choose, you can allow the rain to continue as long as you wish in order to discover the message in that.

These written meditations may be used alone. Because of this, I was more directive than I would be in a group setting. Of course, no matter how direct the guidelines are, your imagery is still a reflection of your inner life at the time of the meditation.

A WORD ABOUT MY INTENTIONS

I greatly value attention to the inner life as a resource for wholeness in relating to the world. In order to develop this resource, it is necessary to practice some of the following disciplines: prayer (private and in communities), dream recording and reflection, meditation, reading (devotional and many types), journal keeping, exercise, attention to responsible diet, imagery exercises, and creativity in many forms of expression and action. Guided imagery meditation on scripture might become one choice among these disciplines. I am not recommending this as *the* method for spiritual integration, but as a very helpful one.

Personally, I find that the type of disciplines which I follow has changed gradually over a period of time. Nine years ago meditation, prayer, and yoga exercises were of primary importance to me. Now, I do the yoga exercises only several times a week, meditate and pray in a different fashion, give more attention to exercise and a responsible diet, and record my dreams. I feel comfortable with the ebb and flow of disciplines.

May you encounter, explore, and grow from your depths . . . as we draw from the same Source.

CHAPTER TWO

REFLECTIONS UPON RELIGIOUS EXPERIENCE

S EVERAL IMPLICIT THEOLOGICAL ASSUMPTIONS UNDERGIRD the type of meditation offered in this book. This chapter is divided into four sections. The first explores briefly religious experience and its relationship to faith. The second section categorizes types of Christian prayer and develops a concept of Christian growth and wholeness. The third section offers a short explanation of the purpose and choice of symbols in imagery meditation. The last section includes personal examples of awareness and growth through imagery meditation.

UNDERSTANDING RELIGIOUS EXPERIENCE

Four widely recognized sources for guidelines in Christian theology are scripture, tradition, experience, and reason. The meditations in this book are based primarily upon *scripture* and *experience*. An individual's tradition will flavor the experience in the meditation, and reasoning will be important as one looks at the images in the meditation and reflects upon how they can be used as guidance in life.

Guided imagery meditations on scripture are particularly exciting because they do not seek a new rigid structure. Rather, they seek to allow meaning, intuition, imagination, and guidance to emerge through the individual. They use the window frame of Christian scripture as a starting point and acknowledge the revelational quality of the symbols therein.

In his book *Hunger for Experience,* John Biersdorf notes five qualities which distinguish *experience*:

1. Experience connects inner and outer reality.
2. Experience is worthwhile not solely as a means to some end, but in and of itself.
3. Experience is sensed to be connected with meaning.
4. Important experience challenges one's view of reality, for this new event must be taken into account.
5. Experience may be spontaneous *or* may be intentionally planned and sought after.[9]

Each of these statements about experience bears directly upon the use of the meditations in this book. Simply doing them, regardless of any later reflections and/or connections, is worthwhile, though seldom as fruitful as when reflection follows. The meditations link the reality of scripture, the inner reality of the meditator, and the external reality of the meditator, as each of those realities is reflected upon. Engaging in meditation is intentional, but also, spontaneous images, thoughts, and feelings are expected to emerge.

John Biersdorf cites Alan Toffler's observation that experience, not goods and services, is the product increasingly offered to consumers by institutions in contemporary society.[10] He underscores his observations, which are based on a detailed study, with his belief that people still do look to religious institutions for "meaning-laden experiences."[11] I think it is essential that religious institutions realize and live up to this demand for vital experience. If religious institutions do not provide adequate "worshipful experiences" in addition to "worship services," people will continue to look elsewhere and seek to find, among the wide opportunities, some coherent form of meaning-experience-making in their lives. It is not my goal merely to keep people in the church; rather it is my conviction that people look to the church for guidance. Religious institutions must recognize their own immense wealth of wisdom, symbolism, and training and use all these assets productively.

Wolfhart Pannenberg, in a sermon at the School of Theology at Claremont, made a distinction between *religious awareness* and *religious experience*. He proposed that the purpose of meditation is to foster an attitude which facilitates religious experience. The attitude itself is not religious experience, but rather religious awareness. Religious experience, in his understanding, is a particular event, occurring at a particular time, which transforms the meaning of the past, indeed all reality, as it is known. This is congruent with Biersdorf's reflection upon *important experience*. Pannenberg explains that the religious experience is not normally understood all at once; it may take a lifetime to figure out. He cites Moses' encounter with the burning bush as an example of a religious experience. Meditation, then, functions to sharpen religious awareness, so that one can be more open to receive religious experience and so that one can then, after an experience, be more sensitive to the understanding of it.

SOME THEOLOGICAL FOUNDATIONS FOR PRAYER

John B. Cobb, Jr., has explained five approaches to Christian spirituality, each of which leads to a different understanding of the purpose of prayer. (1.) If God's will is revealed only through God's word in the Bible, and Christian spirituality is a proper alignment of human will to God's will, then prayer is a preparation of the self to find and obey God's commands as revealed in the Bible. (2.) If rational thought can illumine what seems to be right, then prayer is a means for subordinating selfish impulses to divine purposes as understood through rational conscience. The Bible provides guidelines for thinking clearly. (3.) If whatever happens is seen to be the will of God—in other words, if humans have no free choice—then prayer is seen as a means toward the goal of accepting things as they are, as God's will. (4.) If Spirit is expected to be an "invasive force displacing and replacing normal means of rational reflection and control," then prayer is a form of emptying the self in order to become a channel through which the spirit can flow unhampered. (5.) If the divine is known to be immediately present in the depths or heights of our own being, prayer is a discipline aimed at freeing or releasing the expression of the divine.[12]

Each of these five purposes for what Cobb has labeled *prayer* could likewise be purposes for guided imagery meditation on scripture. Those who look to the Bible as the only revelation of truth may want to approach these meditations with the expectation of getting further in touch with that truth. However, I expect that people who hold this view may have difficulty with personalizing the passages. Those who hold the second attitude, who base trust on rational thought, may find themselves asking how to trust feelings or images. Yet, if they experience these meditations, they could have ample room for reflection afterward. Even those who espouse the third view, believing that everything which happens is the will of God, may use the meditations as a means to achieve the sense of acceptance of God's will. I assume that those who view God as an invasive force would have no theological difficulty with this approach to meditation, though it may seem too structured. Cobb's fifth explanation of Christian spirituality and prayer is most congruent with the view implicit in this approach to meditation.

John Cobb points out that if God is truly incarnate, present in the world, it follows that God is not limited to one human faculty (i.e., reason, emotion, will, imagination) or to one book. Rather, God can be known here and now through an adequate integration of all human faculties. "The wholeness most worth striving for is one in which the maximum complexity of aspects of existence is united."[13] Although Cobb points out that historically Christians have given much greater attention to will than to imagination, he argues that "Indeed, the spirit in all its aspects is peculiarly dependent on imagination."[14] So, for Cobb, the Christian norm is strength and health in all the human aspects, including body, emotions, reason, imagination, intuition, aesthetic sensitivity, will, and spirit. Prayer includes, then, for Cobb, the whole stance of openness to God and responsiveness to the divine call.[15]

Each meditation in this book can be seen as preparation for openness to God as well as a factor in developing responsibility. Even those which seem to be "personal" meditations—for health, for example—are responsible, if they are seen as developing a more holistic stance from which to relate to the world. It is possible that with greater health, one can embody

25

and radiate more fully one's divine potential and hence take responsibility for the giving of that potential to the world.

We have looked at five approaches to Christian spirituality and their accompanying attitudes toward meditation. Process theology fits, it seems to me, into the fifth category. It provides a profound way of understanding God's love, guidance, and interaction with the world, while maintaining the intuitive understanding of a person's free choice. Although not essential to using these meditations, this theological perspective is uniquely harmonious with the approach.

Process theology is a complex metaphysical scheme. Concepts directly derived from process thought are relevant here. Each individual has, in every moment, many options for maximizing his/her unique potential. Of these options, some are more in line with God's aim for the individual, and some are less congruent with this aim. We are free each moment to choose among the various options and free to reject any of them. With this understanding, meditation can be an aid to a more complete understanding of and response to God's aims for us. There is no guarantee that we will know God's primary aims for us, but we can desire to be in harmony with God and seek this consciously. Since God is already seeking to persuade us in our choices (this begins unconsciously), the "turning of our attention" to God allows for even greater comprehension of God's guidance.

Another concept from process thought is that in every moment of our lives each of us influences and is influenced by other persons. We always have free choice, but we choose among the various elements impinging upon us. In each moment God's aim is only one element among many. From this premise, one can see that meditation makes sense for two reasons: it enables us to become more responsive to God's aims, and it functions as conscious influence for ourselves and others. If I inwardly experience a sense of harmony in relation to another person's life or peace towards a national conflict, that embodiment of harmony or peace and that conscious aim for the person or the nation becomes an element in the complex number of influences on that person or nation. Granted, it is only one element, but it can make a difference.

What an exciting and fruitful event meditation can be! It is not useless thinking at all. On the contrary, it is an opening to God's guidance and an intentional gift to others. The meditations in this book are intended to be used both for individual growth and for individual and/or group offerings for the world, with the expectation of growth and change. Although these intentions are made explicit here, your own theological perspective can guide your understanding and use of the meditations.

EXPERIENCING SYMBOLS

Symbols can be unique to an individual and/or have some general, common meaning. Many psychological approaches agree with this basic premise. The Gestalt approach to dream and imagery symbolism stresses the unique meaning of the symbol for the person who has experienced the symbol. Jung, even with his awareness of a huge reservoir of archetypal symbols, expected individual meanings to emerge. Joseph Campbell, who has explored and written about myths and symbols from many cultures, has said that change is so fast today that myths become more and more purely personal. We tend now to find our myths "as we go." However, he points out that there are archetypal symbols which occur in the myths of many cultures. Although we are less influenced by the cultural myths, our own personal symbolism, as it emerges in dreams or images, often expresses the same themes found in the myths of other cultures.[16]

Psychosynthesis uses guided imagery in its group and therapy work and bases the settings upon a general wisdom regarding symbols. Yet this approach also insists that people are unique in their symbolization. Even Artemidorus, in the second century A.D., "hammered away at the point that dream symbols have different meanings in different situations and for different persons."[17]

It seems abundantly clear that people respond differently to a symbol and bring to it and from it a wide variety of meanings. In fact, the same symbol may evoke numerous meanings for an individual over a period of time.

In the meditations, I refer to Jesus as "the Christ." Since a symbol evokes more than the picture of the object referred to, "the Christ" is more clearly a symbol than "Jesus." "The Christ" evokes something beyond thinking of an historical person, although it includes the historical person. "The Christ" can be visualized, if an image appears, in many different ways. For example, the symbol of "the Christ" may appear as male or female, as a person or a star, or as a voice or a memory. Thus the use of the term "the Christ" provides flexibility and openness.

Below are listed some common symbols and their frequently evoked meanings. These are presented to show the purpose behind the choice of the "scene" given in each meditation and because these few symbols can provide guidelines in the creation and use of other guided meditations.

Symbol	Often Evokes
Meadow (grassy area)	a neutral situation or present consciousness
Sun	a center (for action, balance, and source)
	a form of energy (for growth, warmth)
	a form of order, regularity
	the "Higher Self"
	eternal life disengaged from time
Wise person	wisdom, for guidance
	a mediator between where we are and the Higher Self or God

The *meadow, sun,* and *wise person* are the "safest," most nurturing symbols to use.

Plant (flower, seed)	an aspect of growth
Water (pool, beach, river)	an aspect of feeling
	flow of energy (river)
	the unconscious

Symbol *(cont.)*	Often Evokes *(cont.)*
Forest	the unconscious which is near to the surface
Caves (going down)	the lower, deeper unconscious
Mountain (going up)	the higher, superconscious
Gift	facilitates "grounding,"bridging the image experience to daily life (See chapter three, pages 41–43).
House (dwelling)	a view of the personality, or how we see ourself

THREE PERSONAL EXPERIENCES WITH SYMBOLS

During a guided meditation in October, 1975, a *dandelion* emerged for me as a dramatic and important symbol of the qualities which I sought to embody. A dandelion pops up in many places, free to explore widely, carefree of the judgments of others. At that time I needed much inner resilience from the judgment or comments of others as well as from my own internal "oughts." As I occasionally meditated upon the symbol of a dandelion, I found that I truly got in touch with these qualities.

Looking at my journal, I note a few references to the dandelion in meditation. In January the dandelion turned into a chrysanthemum, getting larger, more brilliant. In February the dandelion was in the process of unfolding its petals. In March, in an extended imagery session, I was identifying with the dandelion and was letting my seeds blow far and wide. What is amazing, upon recollection, is that the yellow-flowered stage was the only stage about which I thought for the period from October to March. During that time I might have been preoccupied with blooming. Then I allowed myself to die and shed seeds.

During that period of time a woman whom I had met just once sent me a postcard. Ironically, on the card was a photo of a

29

OPENING TO GOD

dandelion. Soon after this, I found and bought another poster of a dandelion with the quote, "He [sic] who's not busy being born is busy dying" (Bob Dylan).

These images accurately reflect the process which I underwent during the year. I moved from great uncertainty to tentative unfolding to a desire and strength to "shed some seeds."

The dandelion has been a persistent and lasting symbol for me. That is not "good" or "bad." It is simply so. One may have a symbol which keeps emerging or may have many different symbols. It has been important for me not to get attached to the dandelion symbol. I am ready for it to cease its importance when it does. I would limit my needed growth if I became too attached to it. I do not recall meditating with it for several months now. Maybe it is past.

Once while leading a meditation I saw a plot of earth, just being tilled or cultivated. Nothing had been planted, and the time for planting was ripe. That message was confrontive, and I hurt to realize my barren feeling at the time. Yet, the insight beckoned me forward.

On another occasion I led a large group of chaplains (mostly men) in a weekend workshop on spiritual growth. While leading the meditation "Getting a Sense of Your Growth" (number 19) on the second day of the workshop, a seed grew for me in my imagination into an *artichoke*. It was a beautiful purple color, but prickly! Then, it changed into a soft foxglove. (I had just seen both artichokes and foxgloves on a trip to the Pacific Northwest.) I mellowed and felt grace-filled when that change took place. I shared my image with the group and explained the meaning it had for me.

I had attended many workshops as a participant the previous year. The meditations and workshops that I had led were moderately received. Now, I was being looked up to and put at a distance. Some of this was due to my being in the role of the leader; some of it was due to my being one of the few women present; but some of it was due to my own barriers and distancing. I was trying to break through the barriers to become more comfortable with them, more gentle somehow. The image of the prickly flower turning into a soft one enabled me to recognize the conflict. It also helped me to facilitate the actual change in me as the workshop progressed.

These three examples all relate to seeds. They reveal some of my thoughts and feelings during the year. Accepting those as they are, I share them with you. I remain enthusiastically open to your sharing wherever you are, too.

CHAPTER THREE

GUIDELINES FOR USING THESE MEDITATIONS

PREPARATION FOR MEDITATION

T O FACILITATE RELAXATION, EACH OF the meditations in this book begins with the instruction to take three or more slow, deep breaths. There are many good techniques for relaxation. One popular and effective technique is to move through your body in your imagination, relaxing each part and feeling it relax while concentrating upon it. An alteration of this is to tense the area of the body, then relax it, again focusing upon the relaxation. This method is included in the meditation found on page 76. I recommend *The Well Body Book* or *Getting Clear* for additional relaxation exercises.[18]

Most approaches to meditation put an emphasis upon correct posture. The very straight, upright posture, with head above the spine, maximizes one's ability to stay alert and minimizes distractions from the body. Sitting cross-legged, in a half or full lotus, or sitting in a chair is fine. The important thing to remember is to sit straight. There are good sources for precise directions on sitting.[19] Some people recline to do imagery meditation; however, it is very easy to fall asleep in that position.

Please turn to any of the meditations in Part Two and note the several sections of each meditation. If you are meditating alone, you will probably want to read the passage, the biblical note, and the "For Your Meditation" sections before doing the meditation. You could then read through the meditation several times, close your eyes, and do the meditation according to your memory. It does not need to be precise. Or, you may want to read the meditation into a tape recorder and play it back for yourself. If you do this, be careful to read very slowly. Feel free to turn the tape machine off and on while you meditate, to give yourself whatever time you need before the next spoken words. Another method would be to read a small section of the meditation; close your eyes and experience that. Open your eyes and read the next phrase; close your eyes and experience that, and so on.

If a group, either small or large, is participating in meditation, the leader can read the biblical passage and begin the meditation, or read the biblical passage and share the biblical note and/or "For Your Meditation" before beginning the meditation itself. I have discovered that groups which discuss the biblical meanings of the passage first seem to get more involved in the meditation. They seem to have become more "at-one-with" the scene. Also, I think they are freer to let go of the biblical meanings, once verbalized, and more open to let occur what happens for them. Sometimes, for instance in a sermon, the flow occurs more smoothly if you simply say, "I'd like for you to close your eyes and join me in a guided meditation. . . ." This is occasionally more effective than spending time and attention explaining the background information.

I encourage you to change these meditations, to explore in order to find what works best for you. There are many other meaningful passages to develop into meditations. You may want to explore some of these. I have found that the more visual passages of scripture are better resources for imagery meditation. Once I asked people to image loving God "with all your heart, with all your soul, with all your mind, and with all your strength" (Mark 12:30). I thought that would be a terrific meditation on wholeness. But, it simply was not concrete enough. A number of people felt frustrated. On the other hand, to ask people to see a seed grow or to find a hidden treasure is quite precise, simple, concrete, and most often easy to follow.

Because all of one's psyche is available for every meditation, something out of the distant past or the deep unconscious, something strange, confrontive, or threatening could emerge with any meditation. However, some scenes are more inclined toward nurture than others. I have chosen "safer" passages to include in this book. By "safer passages," I mean symbols and settings which generally evoke nurturing, non-threatening, present or future-oriented experiences rather than confrontive,

33

unconscious, or past-oriented experiences. I have not included a meditation on the crucifixion, for example. Although a meditation upon the crucifixion could be insightful, it is best reserved for a practiced meditator, within a group or in therapy. The meditations "In Time of Trouble" (number 16) and "Meditation Upon Saying Good-bye" (number 29) may lead to expressions of grief, anger, and loneliness. They are wisely used with discretion.

If you create your own meditations, attention to this safety factor would be advisable. It would also be helpful to read the short symbolism section or to research elsewhere the symbols involved in the meditation that you are creating.

Aside from the safety factors in the choice of symbols and scenes for meditation, we all have a safety factor within. We have a beautiful regulating system within us which protects us from the conscious awareness of that which we are not yet ready to face. If we do not want to face something, we are likely to fall asleep, forget, or just not see the connections in what is being said in our imagery.

In the meditation process, grief, anger, love, guilt, compassion, sadness, and joy may emerge if the meditator is willing to experience these emotions. The decision to face the many facets of our humanness is a very significant one for each of us. I want to make clear that I think that facing confrontation, threatening dreams or images, and such is important for wholeness. It is not necessary to be overly cautious with meditation. However, it is wise to get in touch with our resources of strength before seeking deliberately to open up the more vulnerable areas.

It is valuable to note the various physiological effects of meditation. Generally, one's oxygen consumption, respiratory rate, heart rate, blood pressure, and muscle tension decrease and alpha waves increase with various types of meditation. This is a clear indication that meditation offers health benefits for many people. I would recommend reading *The Relaxation Response* by Herbert Benson for additional information on this subject.[20] His book is short, eclectic, and easy to read.

Those who are leading a group may discover that these meditations can take longer than expected. I once planned to use the allegory of Jesus and the true vine as an opening meditation for a two-hour group meeting. The meditation took one and one-half hours before we even started the rest of the agenda! However, a meditation on the Resurrection morning experience was done in three to five minutes with five hundred people. It was the opening meditation on the last day of a Methodist Annual Conference. Granted, I felt rushed, but some people shared that they became quite relaxed and found significant value in that short meditation. If you have a time limit, you may want to rehearse the meditation and get quite clear how you are going to use it. The meditations may be expanded or contracted. To shorten the time, some content could be deleted. This would be preferable to hurrying excessively.

Likewise, the individual meditator should be careful to have enough time, or again, limit the meditation itself. Often it is helpful to set a timer in the next room (if you meditate indoors) so that you do not worry whether you are taking too long.

Participants in group meditation experiences have sometimes commented, "I needed more time. You went too fast." Some, but not as many, have said it was too slow. It is important to allow sufficient silence at the pauses. I always do the meditation myself while I am leading it. In this way, I have at least my own pacing to follow. Alone, or in a group, allow time at the end of the meditation simply to sit in silence.

The most facilitative attitude for meditation is one of acceptance towards whatever emerges. As a leader, the attitude of "intrigued delight" at what occurred for the others fosters a non-judgmental, non-analytic acceptance. It is important for each person to ask, "How does that relate to my life?" For example, one person reflected upon "the changing seasons" in a meditation without making any verbal connection to his life experience. When asked this question, he readily saw that he was "changing seasons" in his profession. Although gentle guidance from the leader is often helpful, the message of the meditation needs, as a rule, to emerge from the person her/himself.

Even after I was convinced of the benefits of meditation, I encountered enormous resistance in myself to sitting down and

35

doing it regularly. I found that reading the newspaper, recording dreams, exercising, and even putting my home in perfect order, not to mention my job, were far more essential to get done first. I went through a phase of reflecting on our society's overemphasis upon accomplishment, in distinction from dynamic being, for a long while. What finally broke through some of the resistance was a commitment for six weeks to a biofeedback meditation. A machine was attached weekly, so the results were obvious. After the six-week period I still needed to face the resistance—and still do; however, the experience of daily meditation reduced my resistance. I felt the worth in my body in addition to believing in the worth with my reason.

There are many types of resistances. Things may change in my life; I may grow; my attitudes may alter. Am I willing for this to occur? I may see parts of myself that I have not faced before. (It is interesting that, although people tend to fear facing negative parts of themselves, they are generally surprised to find much hidden beauty and strength.) Am I willing to look? Or, I may resist believing there is any value to meditation, so I prove that to myself!

Several people who live with others have mentioned a problem with finding a place to meditate. For a few, the bathroom is an adequate compromise. However, the most beneficial (and often the most difficult) solution is to tell the people with whom you live how important meditation is for you, or that you have chosen to commit yourself to it. It is valuable to seek acknowledgment of and respect for your decision.

EIGHT SPECIAL GUIDELINES

The following guidelines are good for presentation to a group prior to the group meditation experience. Even for a group which meditates regularly, occasional discussion of these may be wise to refresh people's memories. If meditations are used in worship, it might be helpful to suggest a few guidelines to the congregation before each meditation. Persons who meditate alone will probably want to read through them a few times.

1. *On "seeing"*: Although many people "see" when they do

imagery exercises, some people simply "get a sense" of the scene without a clear picture. Even people who experience "seeing" may or may not see as clearly as if a screen were on the underside of their eyelids. Some people "hear" or "smell" or "feel" in the imagery scenes. Simply be open to what emerges.

2. *On practice:* Practice at imagery does generally lead to clearer "seeing" or "sensing."

3. *On being OK:* It is important not to feel required to "obey" the meditation guide words. If you want to imagine yourself standing on your head when the meditation guide says to imagine sitting down, choose which to do. You may depart a great deal from the *form* of the meditation, or you may stay very close to the form. There is only one right way—your way.

4. *On "nothing" happening:* If you think nothing is happening, please check out what that nothing is. You may be seeing a color, experiencing a sense of frustration, be in touch with anger or resistance to the meditation or to a person, or daydreaming about things to do. Acknowledging this may lead to insight and/or to refocusing upon the meditation itself.

5. *On asking for assistance:* You can bring in assistance or guidance by imagining a friend or "wise person" joining you in the scene. You can imagine yourself equipped with a flashlight if the scene is dark, breathing gear if you are under water, track shoes, crash helmet, food or drink, whenever you want. Since you are creating your scene, you are free to provide yourself with whatever you need. The people of the Senoi tribe of Malaysia use techniques such as this in their work with dreams.[21]

6. *On attachment:* It is best not to get attached to the images that emerge. If you do not feel good about them, continue until you feel more resolved, or feel free to do the meditation again. If you are especially fond of an image, be alert to recognize when it has served its purpose for you, and be ready to let it go.

7. *On debriefing and grounding:* Debrief afterwards. This can

be done in triads in a large group. Three is a good number, for it reduces the possibility that one may think, "I did it wrong," as might be the case in dyads. Or, if you are alone, debriefing can be accomplished through writing in a journal.

8. *On succeeding:* Please do not worry about succeeding, competing, or being appropriate. Simply let go of yourself, and let whatever happens express itself.

WHAT HAPPENS DURING MEDITATION

In my experience with leading others in imagery meditation, a few common phenomena have emerged which may be instructive.

1. A person may fall asleep, generally awakening at the end of the meditation. Or, a person may hear part of the meditation words and simply have no recall of the other parts. There are several reasons this may occur:

    (a) Some persons may suddenly relax, and having previously formed the habit of falling asleep whenever they are that relaxed, they fall asleep while meditating. The path between the conscious and the unconscious is more accessible the more it is traversed either through dream recall or imagery work.

    (b) Some may not have gotten enough sleep!

    (c) Some may already have enough on their mind so that they do not need/want any more input. (Perhaps they are investing a lot of energy into a crisis or creative project.)

    (d) Some may be unwilling to face the topic or material that is emerging (or could emerge) right now in their lives. (For example, being unwilling to acknowledge love for someone because that does not fit into their self-image; or not being ready to go through grief over a loss.)

    (e) Some may resist the leader or something about the situation.

    I respect all the reasons. These factors can occur over and over for many of us. In fact, we can be grateful we have this built-in safety factor. However, we can also grow by looking at the reason for falling asleep.

2. A person may experience going ahead of the meditation, that is, doing in one's imagery what is suggested soon afterward in the verbal or written instruction.

3. A person may see scenes from his/her past when asked to see a meadow, seashore, or mountain. Another person may imagine scenes he/she has never seen. Both of these are all right. I have found that some Southern Californians have difficulty imagining a meadow or a wilderness, so I occasionally change the words to grassy area and deserted area. When I was in Iowa for a year, I encountered a few Mid-Westerners who had difficulty with beach scenes. Feel free to adapt and to laugh.

4. Encountering Jesus or Mary seems to bring mixed responses. Some people are unable to talk to them in the imagery. Others have sexual fantasies. Some suddenly become concerned about how they look. What is important is to recognize what does happen in the imagery and then to reflect upon how that does or does not relate to one's conscious life.

5. Often people say they did not want to return either to the beginning scene of the meditation (which is most often requested) or, more commonly, to the wakeful state. The leader may simply acknowledge that and suggest that the person reflect on the reason for this within the particular meditation. It is important that people return to the wakeful state after each meditation. If they choose to continue with their meditation by entering into the meditation state again, fine. One returns to the scene at the beginning of the meditation because that is normally a neutral place. The person is brought back to that neutrality, not left in a deep place or an ecstasy.

6. People are generally more shy about sharing what they have labeled negative comments or unusual occurrences, such as falling asleep, not hearing, not getting into the meditation, or having a sexual fantasy. I strongly encourage at least some verbalization of "negatives"; people need

39

to know that this is all right. However, I also try not to push the privacy which a person chooses to maintain. I simply like to make clear a willingness to listen.

7. Some people do not like ending with "Open your eyes." Occasionally I say, "Amen." Frankly, I do not know what phrase to use. Perhaps a nice bell would be most appropriate. A bell is used in Arica meditation, zen meditation, and in many disciplines.

8. An amazingly large number of people say that it did not occur to them to bring in assistance (wise person, friend, flashlight, food, etc.). However, people are tremendously creative in working through dilemmas encountered in imagery meditation. It is best for the leader to remember to state the possibility of bringing in assistance *prior* to the meditation. However, it is an awkward guideline to understand until one has already been in a scene in which this type of assistance is needed.

9. I have occasionally included details which were limiting and not necessary. I once called the gardener in the allegory of Jesus as the true vine, a "he." One male in the group had a female gardener. I said, "See the grapes" in that same meditation, but several people had different fruit on their vines. Now I repeat the word *gardener* without using a pronoun, and I say *fruit* rather than *grapes*. In one group, five out of eight people had difficulty planting a seed in sand. I had suggested that they were at the seashore in the parable of the self-growing seed. Each of the five found a creative solution to their logical dilemma, so their meditation was fine and productive. However, now I suggest that people go wherever they want to plant the seed, so that they can more easily find the appropriate soil and setting. Attending to these details is not a difficult problem or a problem at all, if people realize that they do not need to obey the guiding words. However, the leader can minimize the potential inner logical problems by keeping the guiding words as open as possible, whenever doing so stays within the intent of the meditation. Specific details are valuable for getting

into a scene, but there is a fine line between unguided free association and over-guided structuring.

10. One fantastic and fun observation has been the sense of reality ascribed to the meditation scenes. People say, "When I was on the path . . ."; they seldom say, "When I imagined myself to be on the path. . . . " This excites me, for the physical world is one of many realities in which we are already living, yet we seldom affirm the value of these other realities.

DEBRIEFING AND GROUNDING

Debriefing, expressing what occurred either to others or in a journal, is valuable to the guided meditation process. If we do not verbalize or write out what occurred, we are very likely not only to forget the images, but more importantly, to miss the messages.

Ann Faraday's *The Dream Game* has many suggestions for gleaning insight from dreams, suggestions which can easily be applied to imagery experiences. One of Faraday's major insights is that images which emerge may relate to three levels of meaning. First, an image may be a direct message about the external world. For example, in the meditation on the hidden treasure, (number 1) I may see a library book which, in my external life, is due or overdue. The message could be: "Remember the book!" The second level of meaning is an inner message about the external world. An example at this level might be that I discover that I feel anger, love, or grief as I encounter the image of a person whom I know in the meditation on the "Many Mansions" scripture passage (number 29). I receive information about my feeling regarding the person. The third level of meaning is based entirely upon the inner dimension. The imagery at this level refers to me, or aspects of myself. The meditation on the parable of the seeds (number 4) might bring forth images which refer to parts of myself: the child, dancer, compulsive listmaker, dedicated friend, rebellious seeker.

An image in a meditation can relate to more than one level of meaning at the same time. For example, I may see myself with irritated skin in the healing at the pool meditation (number 6).

41

That may be a message on the first level, telling me a fact about my world. It may be informing me to take care of my skin. On the second level, the message may be, "Something is getting under your skin!" That is a message about my internal response to an external event. If it is a message on the third level, it relates entirely to my internal growth. Perhaps it is reflecting an irritating barrier which I place between myself and others. The message may be clearly at one level only; however, occasionally the message makes sense on two or three levels simultaneously. I may truly be getting skin irritations because I erect irritating barriers between myself and others, which then lead to my letting their reaction to me "get under my skin"! Faraday also points out the tendency of the unconscious to play word games or to pun. Perhaps the image above tells me I am getting irritated over my need to be "skinny" . . . or irritated over a decision whether to go "skinny dipping"! Obviously, the guidance in these imagery meditations is not always direct. It is important to *reflect* in order to get the message.[22]

Discussion following a meditation allows for reflection upon theological issues which may arise. There may be several views toward healing, for example, which are shared and explored. The depth in sharing of ideas, feelings, and experiences after these meditations is sometimes amazing. People become open and trusting in a way that I have seldom seen—even compared to groups which use trust exercises to facilitate sharing.

Grounding is a term which I encounter most often in counseling work. A person may have a tremendous feeling or experience a high or find a resolution in a meditation. However, it is possible that the experience does not affect the external lifestyle of the person if it is left to the short period of meditation itself. Grounding puts the insight or experience into concrete form, enabling the person to understand it more clearly.

One of the simplest forms of grounding is drawing. Getting the inner picture out and on paper helps concretize the experience. If the drawing is placed in a frequently observed location, it can act to reinforce the qualities within the meditation. For example, a dandelion has become an important symbol for me, as I explained in the section on my personal experiences with symbols. Now a photo of a dandelion is in my living room, and a poster is in my office. The qualities which I seek to embody, and which I found in the dandelion in my original imagery, continue to be reinforced each time I see either of these symbol pictures.

Another grounding technique is to ask the question, "What am I going to do about this in my life?" or, "What does this say as guidance?" Ann Faraday suggests that people state in a few sentences, "The meaning of my dream is . . ." after sufficient reflection has taken place. That is sound advice for meditation as well.

There are many ways to ground these meditations creatively. Some ideas are listed after each meditation. They include drawing murals with a group; acting out the scene of the meditation, as if in a play; sculpturing some image; and making various appropriate crafts. Adults are usually more inclined to draw if the leader passes out paper in advance, stating at that time that the group will draw after the meditation. Also, if the paper is large, this seems often to add to the enthusiasm.

Not long ago, as I walked through some forests in the Pacific Northwest, I was surprised by the amount of root exposure. It occurred to me that as we debrief, we are exposing some of our "roots,"—which give us support, strength, nourishment, and run deep within us. Although exposing roots is healthy, it makes sense to use discretion in reserving some depth, allowing it to remain unexposed. Each person knows what is a treasure within her/him that is not ripe for disclosure. It is necessary to respect this treasure—even though sharing many roots is healthy and growth-producing.

If these meditations are used in a worship setting, there are a few ways to debrief: (1.) Take time to let two or three people share during the service. (2.) Ask that each person turn to a neighbor and debrief. (3.) Encourage people to draw their images or write what occurred. (If no paper is prepared in advance, even the registration cards can be used for this.) (4.) Make a verbal commitment to be available for working with anyone who feels the need to talk, after the service, or soon. (5.) Ask each person to commit her/himself to sharing her/his experience with someone that day.

43

Some people will say that they had a "bad" experience. I seek to draw out both what occurred and why they have labeled it bad. From my perspective, I have not heard one experience yet which I would consider bad. Some were unpleasant or frightening, but even those were constructive for integrative growth. If you encounter such a "bad " experience yourself or while working with others, here are several suggestions that you can make or follow yourself: (1.) Encourage the person to continue to reflect upon the meaning. (2.) Encourage her or him to get back into the scene and continue in it, bringing in any assistance she/he may want, until a resolution emerges. For instance, if a person experienced seeing her/himself disappear, die, or become weird-looking, let her/him discover a way to "reappear," "come back to life," or "return to normal appearance." In this way she/he can still explore the meaning of the dying (dying to the "old" self, dying to a habit, letting go of the past, dying to a relationship) and yet also experience the new life beyond that symbolic death. (3.) Check out responses from others to this "bad" image.

Some people prefer concentrative meditation upon an object; some people prefer concentration upon "nothing." Still others prefer more expressive meditation, such as guided imagery meditation or movement meditation. In choosing your style of meditation, it is wise to aim toward balance. If you seldom use imagery intentionally, meditation with imagery can be especially balancing. If you image a great deal and work with your dreams, you might find a more concentrative meditation to be better for balance. Guided imagery meditation lends itself to inclusion within a program of meditation of other forms. One should discontinue use of a certain type of meditation if, after having tried it for a sufficient period of time, it just does not feel right.

If the meditations are used in a worship service, the location can vary within the liturgy. The index on page 137 offers ideas for use as parts of the liturgy. One might consider using this type of meditation about every other week in a regular church setting.

The indexes list the meditations according to: use in daily life, use in worship, symbols, meditation titles, and biblical passages. I expect that these listings will be helpful to those choosing a meditation for a specific purpose or setting.

For those persons who will be leading group meditations, I would like to offer a personal opinion. I believe that it is distasteful to "preach" through a guided meditation. That is, if I have a point to make, I prefer to make it directly. I try to use the meditation for experiencing something parallel to the topic, with full trust in people's own discovery. For example, I would not suggest what the Christ or Mary says to a person in the meditation (except when that is the biblical quote). I try to provide the setting for the dialogue to emerge within each individual.

I want you to be encouraged to begin to lead these meditations. One extremely helpful method which I have used for improvement is to tape the meditations which I lead. Then, I listen to the tapes and see where I would make changes the next time. Although this method is time-consuming (and often painful), it certainly has its merits. The largest obstacle I had to overcome was the barrier to hear fully what people said. When I got to the point of not caring so much what people thought of me or my leadership, I was able to listen to their comments and consequently grow, myself.

PART TWO

THE MEDITATIONS

HOW TO USE
THE MEDITATIONS

Y OU MAY WANT TO START with the first meditation and go
through the meditations in numerical order. The meditations have been arranged with this in mind. The ones near the
beginning are easier to image. They are also more evocative of
inner resources for strength. The ones which tend to elicit more
struggling occur later. Rather than being organized by theme
(i.e., relationships, developing a quality, healing, service to
others, reflection upon one's life) they are listed so that the
themes rotate. I hope this will provide a balanced approach to
growth. However, even though attention has been given to
ordering these for one who wants to begin and work through
them progressively, I expect that these will be more useful if
they are used in relation to a particular need or setting. Therefore, the Indexes offer several ways to choose a meditation. You
may want to turn to the Indexes now to notice the options
provided.

The biblical quotes are taken from *The New English Bible*,[23]
with exception of Number 27, which is found in *The Gospel
According to Thomas*.[24] The "Biblical Notes" are highly dependent upon *The Interpreter's Bible*.[25] Many of the ideas offered in
the "Comments on Debriefing and Use" are especially for group
use, but most of the ideas are feasible even if you are doing these
alone.

It would be advisable for you to read *all* of chapter three prior
to doing any of these meditations. Listed below is a summary of
steps for using the meditations.

MEDITATING ALONE:

1. Choose your place to meditate. Be sure you have freedom to concentrate.
2. Decide how much time you have to meditate. You might set a timer nearby, but not so close to be a distraction. After you decide, let go of your concern for the time.
3. Choose the meditation you will use. Either move progressively through the book or browse through the Indexes to find a meditation which suits your present needs. Instead, you may repeat one you have already experienced which feels unfinished or which was especially meaningful.
4. Sit with a very upright posture, straight, yet relaxed.
5. Remind yourself of the Eight Special Guidelines.
   (a) You may "see," but you may simply get a sense of the scene.
   (b) Practice does increase your ability to image.
   (c) No matter what happens in your imagery, that is OK.
   (d) If you think "nothing" is happening; ask yourself what that "nothing" is.
   (e) If you ever feel the need for assistance in your meditation, bring it into your imagery. You can bring in a helper, friend, or whatever you need.
   (f) No matter what happens—"good" or "bad"—this is simply what is occurring now. It can and will change.
   (g) Debrief or ground the experience after the meditation.
   (h) Do not worry about succeeding, competing, or being appropriate. Simply let go and let the meditation move along as it will.
6. Take a few slow, deep breaths to relax.
7. Read the first three sections of the meditation (the Biblical Reading, the Biblical Note, and the For Your Meditation Section). These are included in each meditation.
8. Decide if there are any special areas on which you expect to work during the meditation.
9. Take a few more slow, deep breaths to relax.
10. Do the meditation. (Use a method below or one you create.)
    (a) Alternate reading and closing your eyes in order to visualize.

(b) Read the whole meditation several times, then visualize it as you remember it, without worrying whether you include every detail.

(c) Tape-record the meditation in advance (with a slow reading) and turn on the tape-machine now.

11. Sit in silence after the meditation.

12. Debrief and ground your experience.

    (a) Write in a journal.

    (b) Draw some part of the meditation.

    (c) Ask yourself how it relates to your life situation now.

    (d) Look at the three levels of meanings.

    (e) Share your reflections with a friend.

    (f) Decide if you want to continue to work on something which emerged and how you will do that.

LEADING A GROUP

1. Reflect upon the setting in which this will be done (the number of people, time of day, seating arrangement, acoustical situation, etc.).

2. Decide how much time you have to do the whole meditation (the introduction, the meditation, and the debriefing).

3. Choose the meditation to meet the needs of the people within that setting. The Indexes offer guidelines for this.

4. Make any changes in the meditation which seem appropriate. Rehearse reading it, or think it through so that you can lead it with only a few notes or no notes.

5. Call the group's attention to as many of the Eight Special Guidelines as is appropriate for the setting:

    (a) You may "see," but you may simply get a sense of the scene.

    (b) Practice does increase your ability to image.

    (c) Do not worry about "obeying" the leader. If you do not follow the leader's words, that is OK.

    (d) If you think "nothing" is happening, ask yourself what that "nothing" is.

    (e) If you ever feel the need for assistance in your meditation, bring it into your imagery. You can bring in a helper, friend, or whatever you need.

OPENING TO GOD

(f) No matter what happens—"good" or "bad," this is simply what is occurring now. It can and will change.

(g) Debriefing will take place after the meditation. (You might explain how.)

(h) Do not worry about succeeding, competing, or being appropriate. Simply let go and let the meditation move along as it will.

6. Pass out paper or anything you may use for the debriefing.

7. Call the group's attention to posture. Suggest a very upright posture, straight, yet relaxed.

8. Read or discuss the biblical passage, the biblical note, the For Your Meditation section, and any further ideas you have on the passage or meditation.

9. Lead the group in a few slow, deep breaths for relaxation.

10. Lead the meditation, slowly, in one of the following fashions.

(a) Read from this book.

(b) Lead it from notes you have taken from the written meditation.

(c) Lead it from your memory of doing it several times yourself, without worry about being exact.

(d) On rare occasions, it may be appropriate to play a pre-recorded tape of the written meditation.

11. Be silent after the meditation.

12. Debrief and ground the experience.

(a) Share verbally.

(b) Draw, make a mural, or creatively express the experience in some other way.

(c) Write in individual journals.

(d) Ask how the meditation relates to their immediate life situation.

(e) Recall the three levels of meanings.

(f) Lead the individuals or the group as a whole to decide upon further action.

(g) Check for any unfinished business—things which people have not yet mentioned but would like to.

52

1

Finding a Buried Treasure

Reading: "The kingdom of Heaven is like treasure lying buried in a field. The man who found it, buried it again; and for sheer joy went and sold everything he had, and bought that field" (Matthew 13:44).

Biblical Note: The "hidden" treasure (which is already present) is the kingdom of God in this parable. The kingdom of God is so joyful that Jesus believed that a person would give up all else to participate in it.

For Your Meditation: This meditation is primarily focusing upon the treasure. Let yourself be open to *any* treasure which might appear. Meditation Number 24 picks up the theme of selling all else in order to have the treasure.

Meditation: Take three slow, deep breaths and let yourself relax. . . .* Get a sense of yourself walking along a beach. . . . Feel the sand beneath your feet, its temperature and texture. . . . Feel the warmth of the sun radiating upon your body. . . . Pay attention to what is around you on the beach. . . . as you walk, notice something that looks like a disturbance in the sand, and push away the sand to find a buried treasure. . . . Do whatever you need to do to uncover that treasure. . . . Now as you open it, become aware of what is hidden within. . . . Spend whatever time you need observing, becoming aware of, talking with or being with that treasure. . . . Let yourself participate in any way you want with that treasure. . . . Be aware of the other things in your life and how they relate to this treasure. . . . What is important?. . .You may encounter Christ and talk about

---

*Ellipsis marks in the meditation indicate appropriate places to pause.

this. . . . If you need to bring in other people or things, do that. . . . Follow through with this treasure in any way that feels right for you now. . . . Find some way to bring back with you a symbol of this treasure. . . . Walk back up the beach again, aware of the sand, the water, and the warm sun. . . . When you feel ready, open your eyes.

Comments on Debriefing and Use: The treasure may have been for you a talent which has lain dormant, a quality which you wish to develop, a gift which you can give to the world, an awareness of the "kingdom of God," or any number of other possibilities. You may find, experiencing this meditation several days in a row, that you discover several different treasures. Or, you may get more thoroughly in touch with the same treasure, if that is what keeps appearing. You may want to limit "the treasure" to a symbol or awareness of the kingdom of God. The reason I have not done this here is that the kingdom of God may be an abstract notion to some, so it is difficult for them to visualize. The notion of "treasure" usually evokes a very concrete and positive finding, which would likely be a part of the kingdom.

If you did not find a treasure or if you found nothing within it, then simply accept that this is what occurred for you just now. Allow yourself first to understand your feelings in not finding a treasure. Later you might choose to do the meditation again.

There are many exciting debriefing activities possible for children in this meditation. You could make a box (or use a shoe box) and put your hidden treasure within the box in the form of a picture, a symbol, or in words.

2

Along Your Life Path

Reading: "You see," said Naomi, "your sister-in-law has gone back to her people and her gods; go back with her." "Do not urge me to go back and desert you," Ruth answered. "Where you go, I will go, and where you stay, I will stay. Your people shall be my people, and your God my God" (Ruth 1:15-16).

Biblical Note: After the death of her husband, Ruth chose to leave her country and people in order to be with her mother-in-law in a foreign land with a different religion. That choice was an important one in Ruth's life.

For Your Meditation: It is valuable to think of our journey through life as a guided path. We find encouragement in knowing that God's pulls are always being offered. Each of us made choices yesterday. Today we are truly making choices anew.

Meditation: Sit quietly and take at least three slow, deep breaths. . . . Get a sense of yourself being on your life path. . . . Notice the kind of path that it is for you and how you are moving along that path. . . . Look back and notice the kind of path on which you have traveled. Let yourself become aware of the decisions and choices you have made. . . . Now become aware of where you are today on your path. Look around and do whatever you need to do to get in touch with where you are today. . . . Now become aware of the path ahead of you. . . . You do not know with any certainty where it leads or the choices that it will offer. Get a sense of yourself being guided or nudged by God to make right choices. . . . You may want to walk ahead on the path and sense yourself moving forward, experiencing this pull toward right decisions. . . . If any particular decision emerges for you, pay attention to it and to your response. . . . Take whatever time you need to continue with as much looking forward as you want. . . . Now remember Ruth and her decision. Let her come into your imagination and communicate with her about her choice and your choices. . . . Now get a sense of the many people throughout the world who are following their unique paths. . . . Let yourself sense an acceptance of these people as they are. . . . You may especially pay attention to those in your family, or those close to you, and feel this acceptance about them. . . . Sense now the potential for right choices being made available to all. Amen.

Comments on Debriefing and Use: If you draw the path and find that some particular part of it is unclear for you, go back into meditation and work out that part of the path. You might act out your meditation, saying aloud, "I am now making this decision," as you had made it in the past. Then move forward to the present and as far toward the future as feels comfortable for you. This meditation could be used for members of a group to get to know each other.

3

Expanding a Quality

Reading: Again he said, "The kingdom of God, what shall I compare it with? It is like yeast which a woman took and mixed with half a hundredweight of flour till it was all leavened" (Luke 13:20-21; see also Matthew 13:33 for parallel version).

Biblical Note: Leaven has been used as a symbol of evil in many of the Jewish writings and elsewhere in the New Testament (see Luke 12:1; Matthew 16:6, 11; Mark 8:15; 1 Corinthians 5:6-8; Galatians 5:9). However, here the reference is to the small amount of yeast necessary to make an enormous amount of dough. This probably was interpreted at the time as a prophecy about the growth of the church and the spreading of the gospel.

For Your Meditation: Think of some quality in your life that you sense needs development. The quality might be patience, compassion, joy, serenity, humor, creativity, or something else which seems to reflect the kingdom of God. In order to decide which quality would be the basis of this meditation, you might become quiet, center in, then allow a quality to emerge. Or, you might look through your journal, if you keep one, and look for a quality you have noted often in your reflections. Quietly think about the wisdom of expanding this quality in your life. Before you meditate, check out the ethical implications of this quality, whether the timing is right, and your sense of commitment to developing it.

Meditation: Take three deep breaths as you sit upright in a comfortable position and allow yourself to relax. . . . Imagine yourself sitting in a comfortable surrounding. This may be your home or any other comfortable setting for you. Look around you to see where you are, what colors, fragrances, and sounds surround you. . . . Now visualize a large bowl of dough in front of you. . . . Put a small amount of yeast into the bowl and follow the process of making bread until the dough rises. . . . Stay in touch with the yeast permeating the entire mass. . . . Visualize baking the bread. . . . As you finally take the bread out of the oven, observe the quality of it. . . .

Now again look at your comfortable surroundings. . . . Remind yourself of the quality which you have chosen to develop. . . . Remember a time when you experienced this quality in some measure in your life. . . . Let yourself experience that quality as you did then. . . . (long pause) Let this be your yeast, and imagine moving through your daily routine, letting this quality permeate that routine. . . . Notice the effect on other people as you radiate this quality. . . . Sit, simply aware of this quality permeating your being and radiating through you and all that you do. . . . When you feel ready, open your eyes.

Comments on Debriefing and Use: Visualizing the yeast in the breadmaking generally helps one to go into the more abstract visualization of living out a quality. If you repeat this meditation, you may find that you want to omit the yeast section and simply visualize the quality, thinking through a day in which you are living that quality more fully.

This would be a good meditation to use in a worship setting for communion or in an event in which a group of people bake bread for their own communion. Slides could be used to show how the bread rises.

A follow-up exercise which is used in Psychosynthesis is to write the quality in the center of a piece of paper and to meditate upon this quality daily. Words which you associate with that quality can be written as spokes to a wheel, with the quality as the hub. Most people who meditate in order to develop a certain quality agree that it takes at least two months to observe that quality truly becoming a central part of their life. Thus, doing this meditation over a period of time would make it far more beneficial.

4

Reflections Upon Your Seeds

Reading: On another occasion he began to teach by the lake-side. The crowd that gathered round him was so large that he had to get into a boat on the lake, and there he sat, with the whole crowd on the beach right down to the water's edge. And he taught them many things by parables.

As he taught he said:

"Listen! A sower went out to sow. And it happened that as he sowed, some seed fell along the footpath; and the birds came and ate it up. Some seed fell on rocky ground, where it had little soil, and it sprouted quickly because it had no depth of earth; but when the sun rose the young corn was scorched, and as it had no root it withered away. Some seed fell among thistles; and the thistles shot up and choked the corn, and it yielded no crop. And some of the seed fell into good soil, where it came up and grew, and bore fruit; and the yield was thirtyfold, sixtyfold, even a hundredfold." He added, "If you have ears to hear, then hear" (Mark 4:1-9; see also Matthew 13:1-9, Luke 8:4-8 for parallel versions).

Biblical Note: The symbol of the sower scattering seed was used occasionally in the ancient world to represent a teacher and the teaching. This parable shows how different hearers respond to the gospel. It is clear that Jesus believed that people could choose to hear and respond.

For Your Meditation: This meditation affirms the past, with its mixed experiences, and the future, with its potential.

Meditation: Take a few deep breaths. Get a sense of yourself on a small hill by a lake. . . . Feel the warmth of the sun. . . . Now, as you look toward the beach, you see people gathered. . . . Notice the Christ standing on a boat, talking to the people. . . . You go down the hill to the shore. . . . As you watch and listen, you hear the Christ talk about seeds which represent how one responds to the gospel. Some seeds fall along footpaths, on the rocky ground, among the thistles, and in good soil. . . . The Christ gives everyone five seeds. . . . Receive your seeds and move away from the crowd, to any place that feels right to sow your seed. . . . Imagine yourself throwing these five seeds, allowing them to land where they will.

The first seed lands upon a footpath. The birds come and eat it up. Allow yourself to reflect upon something in your life that was picked out before it had a full chance to grow. . . . Be aware of your feelings. . . .

The second seed lands upon rocky soil; it takes root, but dies quickly because it has no depth. As you see this seed grow, then die, allow it to represent something in your life that withered because it was not securely rooted. . . . Let yourself feel what occurs. . . .

The third seed lands, grows, but is choked out by thistles. Become aware of something in your life which has been choked out by other interests, activities, values.

Your fourth seed lands, takes root in good soil, grows, and bears fruit. Watch this take place. . . . Now observe what in your life has borne great fruit. Get a sense of that ripe fruit. . . .

Your last seed represents your future. Watch it and allow it to unfold. It may represent an aspect of your life now, as it unfolds in the future, or it may represent something completely new. Allow it to mature. . . . Let the seeds be carried to wherever they want or need to go. . . . Become aware that seeds nurture us and others, far around the world. . . . Sense all these sharings of seeds. Do what you want to do now. Either go back to the hill, finish something with one of the seeds that needs to be finished, or anything else. . . . Become aware of your surroundings, and when you are ready open your eyes.

Comments on Debriefing and Use: It would be excellent to draw the five seeds. If you are in a group, you could prepare a mural with the many seeds, then discuss the drawings with their accompanying meanings.

5

Encountering God— Receiving a Mission

Reading: Moses was minding the flock of his father-in-law Jethro, priest of Midian. He led the flock along the side of the wilderness and came to Horeb, the mountain of God. There the angel of the Lord appeared to him in the flame of a burning bush. Moses noticed that, although the bush was on fire, it was not being burnt up; so he said to himself, "I must go across to see this wonderful sight. Why does not the bush burn away?" When the Lord saw that Moses had turned aside to look, he called to him out of the bush, "Moses, Moses." And Moses answered, "Yes, I am here." God said, "Come no nearer; take off your sandals; the place where you are standing is holy ground." . . . The Lord said, "I have indeed seen the misery of my people in Egypt. I have heard their outcry against their slave-masters. I have taken heed of their sufferings, and have come down to rescue them from the power of Egypt. . . . I will send you to Pharaoh and you shall bring my people Israel out of Egypt." "But who am I," Moses said to God, "that I should go to Pharaoh, and that I should bring the Israelites out of Egypt?" God answered, "I am with you. . . ." (Exodus 3:1-5, 7-8a, 10-11).

Biblical Note: Earlier in his life, Moses showed his readiness to sacrifice for his people. He killed an Egyptian who was beating a Hebrew slave and then fled, finding refuge in the land of Midian. At the time of this passage he has just adjusted to the life of a shepherd. Now he meets God. *Angel* means "messenger," so a messanger of the Lord appeared. The *flame* indicates that God is actually present. Moses is awed, but also receptive. He is modest; therefore, he experiences some doubts and frustrations at receiving this mission, but God promises to be present. It is clear that this is God's project, not one left to Moses, and God enables Moses' modesty to be transformed into the humility of faith.

61

For Your Meditation: You might act out this meditation as well as image it in your mind. I shared this with some teenagers who found a great deal of excitement in the experience of an encounter with God. However, they had a much more difficult time expressing their mission in the world. I decided that a discussion of world *concerns* which they could influence would be valuable before such a meditation.

Meditation: Become quiet and take a few slow, deep breaths. Become aware of yourself as a shepherd walking along tending your flock. . . . You are walking along, and you notice something which catches your attention because of its awe. . . . You turn aside, and as you turn, you hear God speak to you. . . . God speaks your name. . . . You respond. . . . God tells you to take off your shoes, for this is holy ground; you do that. . . . God tells you that God has seen some concern in your life or the life of others. God mentions this and you listen. . . . God informs you that you can do something about it, and you listen. . . . You question what you can do. . . . Allow yourself to ask any questions that you want. . . . Share any doubts that you might feel or any other concerns or hopes. . . . Allow God to reassure you that God is with you always. . . . Allow yourself to sense this. . . . Communicate anything else that feels necessary. When you are ready, finish your dialogue with God and continue herding your flock. . . . As you are tending your flock, think back on what has occurred and let it soak in. . . . When you feel ready, open your eyes.

Comments on Debriefing and Use: Sharing with another person a drawing of the imagery, or making plays, murals, or paintings of the events would all be possibilities for grounding. Be sure to give attention to the guidance received for action.

6

Toward Wholeness and Health

Reading: Later on Jesus went up to Jerusalem for one of the Jewish festivals. Now at the Sheep-Pool in Jerusalem there is a place with five colonnades. Its name in the language of the Jews is Bethesda. In these colonnades there lay a crowd of sick people, blind, lame, and paralysed. Among them was a man who had been crippled for thirty-eight years. When Jesus saw him lying there and was aware that he had been ill a long time, he asked him, "Do you want to recover?" "Sir," he replied, "I have no one to put me in the pool when the water is disturbed, but while I am moving, someone else is in the pool before me." Jesus answered, "Rise to your feet, take up your bed and walk." The man recovered instantly, took up his stretcher, and began to walk (John 5:1-9).

Biblical Note: The man was lying beside the pool, waiting to be the first to jump in after there was a disturbance, or movement in the water. In ancient times there was a superstition that a local divinity was present when there was a disturbance in the water. The Jewish people changed that to indicate that an angel was present, and that the first person able to bathe in the pool would be cured. Since this man was lame, he was never the first person in the pool, for someone always entered the water before him.

For Your Meditation: Think of some particular part of your body in which you would like to have greater health. Or, if you would like to think of this emotionally, intellectually, or spiritually, think of some aspect of your life which you would like to have made more whole.

Meditation: Sit quietly and take a few slow, deep breaths. . . . Allow the tension in your body to be released. . . .

Imagine yourself by a pool of water. . . . Notice what people are with you as you are beside this pool. . . . Notice what the edge of the pool is like. . . . Look at the water and notice the color, the temperature, the texture. . . . Notice the details of this pool. . . . Now become aware of your own body and of a particular area which you would like to be more healthy. . . . Observe the Christ walking toward you, sitting down beside you, and asking you what you are doing. You respond, telling the Christ why you are there. . . . Christ asks you if you want to be made whole. . . . Feel free to interact. Communicate in any way that feels right for you. . . . Decide with the Christ what you are going to do. . . . You may simply get up, affirm your wholeness, and walk on home. Or, you may move into the water and swim around, splashing, and feeling the wholeness cleansing and healing your body. Or, you may come to understand some guidance. . . . Let yourself finish this scene as feels right for you. Stay in touch with the quality of health and wholeness that surrounds the water in this pool, the faith and conviction that you and Christ share. . . . Know that you can return to this setting in your imagination whenever you want. . . . When you are ready, open your eyes.

Comments on Debriefing and Use: This meditation may continue to aid the process of healing within your body, emotions, mind, and spirit. I would suggest using this daily or twice or three times daily if you are working on a major challenge. If this is done in a group, I feel that a discussion of healing is important. It seems to me that we can think of prayer and meditation as facilitating the natural healing and immunizing process of our body rather than as giant pills to bring instant cures. Although I am quite aware that instant cures do occur, I would rather foster a hope which is a trust in healing than a hope which may or may not be shattered by a trust in instant healing.

7

Forgiving and Being Forgiven

Reading: "If, when you are bringing your gift to the altar, you suddenly remember that your brother has a grievance against you, leave your gift where it is before the altar. First go and make your peace with your brother, and only then come back and offer your gift" (Matthew 5:23-24).

Biblical Note: The gift is probably a special sacrifice. The word *brother* would have been interpreted by the original hearers as "fellow Jew." Jesus probably did not mean to limit brother to its meaning today. We can expand the term to mean any person or any living thing.

For Your Meditation: This is a good meditation to do regularly, to discharge pent-up feelings which truly limit your joy in life. This could be especially helpful to do alone just before attending a family gathering or a get-together with friends.

Meditation: Take a few deep breaths to relax and center in. . . . Now get a sense of yourself inside a beautiful temple or sacred place. . . . Notice the structure, the colors, the fragrances, and the people who are there. . . . Allow yourself to absorb the beauty, the dignity, the sense of majesty. . . . Now become aware that you have a gift in your hand. . . . Walk up toward the altar and place the gift upon the altar. While you are there, standing or kneeling, think back to see if there is anyone toward whom you feel anger or resentment or who you think holds anger toward you. . . . Become aware of that anger within you, that resentment, or that unfinished business, whatever it may be. . . . Now walk back down the aisle of the temple or sacred place to go to talk to that person whom you have not forgiven or with whom you do not have peace. . . . Encounter that person and communicate with that person in any way that seems most effective. . . . You can always ask for assistance, if needed, in order to communicate with that person. . . . When you feel ready, go back with your gift to the sacred place or temple and to the altar. . . . Again, reflect to see if there is anyone with whom you have unfinished business. . . . If so, then go out again, find that person and communicate with him or her. . . . Again, go back into the temple and up to the altar with your gift. Become aware again of the majesty within this place and the sense of cleansing forgiveness. Sense God's all pervading love moving through you. Offer your gift at the altar and experience its being accepted. When you feel ready, move out of the temple and into your daily life. . . . When you are ready, open your eyes.

Comments on Debriefing and Use: You may find that it will take you several meditations to get to the point where you feel that you have truly forgiven some people. You may find that when you do this meditation the second or third or fifteenth time, you still find more people whom you have not completely forgiven.

The tension between experiencing anger and experiencing love can be a challenging one. In meditation we can at least work on developing the love that goes beyond conflict. We need to deal with conflicts in the world. However, they work out much better when love is permeating the resolution.

You may draw the temple, the people, or the gift. You may find a tag on the gift which offers some guidance for keeping alert to this love. You might do this meditation actually moving around within the room by yourself. Various people, each with their eyes closed, could do this within a room. Discussion following this would be very valuable. Within a worship setting, this could easily be done as part of the prayer of confession and forgiveness.

8

Calming the Storm Within

Reading: So they cried to the Lord in their trouble,
                    and he brought them out of their distress.
             The storm sank to a murmur
                 and the waves of the sea were stilled.
             They were glad then that all was calm,
                    as he guided them to the harbour they
                    desired.
             Let them thank the Lord for his enduring love
             (Psalm 107:28-31).

Biblical Note: This passage describes the power of God
even as passages in the New Testament refer to Jesus' ability to
deliver people out of storms, literal or figurative (Matthew
8:23-27, Mark 4:36-41, John 6:16-21). Since the Hebrews were
people of the land, the nautical theme in this passage is a
novelty.

For Your Meditation: This meditation may be especially
valuable if you are in a period of stormy times in your life or in
the midst of a particular "storm" during the day. *Harbor* can
represent a "safe place" to which you can return.

Meditation. Take three or more slow deep breaths and
get in touch with the depths within. Now visualize yourself in a
boat . . . . Notice the size and type of boat. . . . Discover who is
with you. . . . Become aware how you feel being there. . . . Now
you notice the water is very troubled, a storm is surrounding
you. . . . Stay in touch with your feelings in this storm. . . . When
you are ready, become aware of the calming presence in your
midst. . . . You might call out to that presence to calm the storm,
or you might simply become aware that the presence is calming
the storm. . . . Let yourself experience that movement from

storm to calm and reflect on how you feel and what is occurring. . . . Now move into the harbor and stay alert to your feelings and thoughts as your boat nudges into its harbor. . . . Before you disembark, look around on the boat for a symbol or image which represents this deep calm for you, and take that symbol with you as you get off the boat. . . . Become aware of your thankfulness for the loving presence enabling that calm. . . . When you feel ready, open your eyes.

Comments on Debriefing and Use: If you had a clear image or symbol to bring back from the boat, draw that or think about that image and how that represents calmness for you. You might draw both the stormy picture and the calm picture. You might hang the pictures in some obvious place to help you to reinforce those experiences. You might also write down how the storm in your particular life right now is affected by this deep sense of calm. Notice any changes in attitude toward the storm in your life. If you had any difficulty or were unable to allow the calmness to occur for you, simply acknowledge that this is where you are right now. Feel free to do this meditation again. Also feel free to write out the stormy feelings.

9

Let Your Light Shine

Reading: "You are light for all the world. A town that stands on a hill cannot be hidden. When a lamp is lit, it is not put under the meal-tub, but on the lamp-stand, where it gives light to everyone in the house. And you, like the lamp, must shed light among your fellows, so that, when they see the good you do, they may give praise to your Father in heaven" (Matthew 5:14-16).

Biblical Note: The light of the world is a phrase which rabbis used when naming God, Israel, or the Torah.

For Your Meditation: Light is a symbol that has been used throughout history to represent the divine, or some aspect of the divine, such as radiance or wisdom.

Meditation: Become quiet and take a few, deep, slow breaths. . . . Now picture yourself in a grassy area . . . . The sun is shining, penetrating through you. . . . You walk through the grassy area, aware of the colors, fragrances, and sights around you. . . . You come to a dwelling of some kind, a structure. . . . Stand before the structure and observe the details from outside. . . . Notice what the door is like, what the structure is made of, what color and texture it is. . . . When you have observed the outside, walk up to the front door, open it, and slowly walk inside. . . . You notice a lamp, and you light it. . . . As you light it, you sense the light move throughout the whole place. That light is illuminating to some extent the whole structure. . . . Stand, observing that lamp, and become aware that you, too, are radiating throughout this place. Identify with the quality of light. . . .

Now look for a place where you could put the lamp to make it shine more brightly throughout this structure. . . . Observe the intensity of the light permeating through the structure. . . . Get a sense of yourself radiating like this light. If there is a place anywhere at all where you can be brighter, like the lamp, go ahead and put yourself there. If you need any assistance to get there, you can ask for any help you need or want. . . . Try to discover what you are doing there, and keep in touch with the quality of light which you are radiating. . . . If you would be brighter by facing in a certain direction, then turn that way. . . . Do whatever you need to do to let your light shine. . . . Look at your surroundings and see how the surroundings are affected by your light.

Bring yourself back to the structure, if you have left. When you feel ready, go back to the grassy area, still keeping in touch with the quality of light that you are radiating. . . . Remember what has occurred for you. . . . When you feel ready, open your eyes.

Comments on Debriefing and Use: A sketch of the lamp in the dwelling and of you in your brightest environment would be valuable.

This would be beautiful as part of a candlelight service in a worship setting. This meditation can be combined with the meditation on feeding the five thousand (number 21), for they both relate vividly to world concerns. This also would be useful if you find yourself in a tense or difficult situation, or perhaps, if you are studying, to gain greater illumination.

10

The Foundation Within Your Home

Reading: "Why do you keep calling me, 'Lord, Lord'—and never do what I tell you? Everyone who comes to me and hears what I say, and acts upon it—I will show you what he is like. He is like a man who, in building his house, dug deep and laid the foundations on rock. When the flood came, the river burst upon that house, but could not shift it, because it had been soundly built. But he who hears and does not act is like a man who built his house on the soil without foundations. As soon as the river burst upon it, the house collapsed, and fell with a great crash" (Luke 6:46-49; see also Matthew 7:21,24-27 for parallel version).

Biblical Note: In Luke, the second house is built on soil, and the stress is on the sturdy construction. Matthew's version seems to emphasize the difference in the choice of locations for the buildings: sand or rock.

For Your Meditation: This meditation is written for reflection about the qualities within your home. A family might experience this meditation together. However, you could change the meditation to refer to your church, an institution, your work environment, or even the places of your vacation. Before you begin, think of some qualities or values which are important to you in the setting you have chosen.

Meditation: Take a few slow, deep breaths and relax. Visualize yourself in some comfortable part of your home. . . . As you get a sense of yourself there, get in touch with some qualities or values you would like to have expressed in your home. Reflect on these as long as you choose. . . . Now slowly walk around your home in your imagination, aware of the feelings you have as you go from room to room. . . . Do this in much detail, perhaps picking up things around your house as you walk; perhaps talking to family members as you move from room to room. . . . Simply experience each room in your home. . . . Stop in a place of your own choosing. . . . Recall the feelings you had as you went around your home. . . . Pay attention to any images, ideas, or feelings that arise. . . . Recollect the qualities or values which are important to you. . . . Walk around your home again slowly in your imagination and see the rooms expressing these values more fully. Notice any changes which occur. . . . Now imagine a storm hitting your home. . . . It may be a physical storm or a storm of problems. . . . Observe how your home endures the storm. .·. . Bring in any assistance you need to repair or rebuild any damages, or even to rebuild the foundation. . . . When it is rebuilt, think again of the qualities or values permeating your strengthened home. . . . Maintain calm for a while. . . . When you feel ready, open your eyes.

Comments on Debriefing and Use: You could draw four pictures of your home: how it looked at first, how it was with the values or qualities strengthened, how it appeared after the storm, and finally how it changed with any repairs. This could lead into much discussion, at each of the stages. If adequate debriefing is allowed, this meditation, used in a group, takes at least an hour.

11

Blooming

Reading: Let the wilderness and the thirsty land be
glad,
let the desert rejoice and burst into flower
(Isaiah 35:1).

Biblical Note: In this scripture passage, the people are
promised a joyful return to Zion on a highway prepared by God.
The highway will run through an arid desert. The desert referred to was probably the Syrian desert, which lay between the
people in exile and their homeland. The wilderness may refer
more specifically to the area of the Dead Sea. This first verse is a
burst of song, as God's creative power enables nature to break
forth with new life and beauty.

For Your Meditation: You might want to choose this
meditation when you are in a "wilderness" or "dry place" in your
life. Or, you may choose this simply to become more aware of life
blooming through you.

Meditation: Become quiet, close your eyes, and take a
few, slow, deep breaths. . . . Imagine yourself in a meadow. Feel
how tall the grass is; feel it against your legs. . . . Experience
yourself walking through this meadow. . . . . Look around you to
see what else is there. . . . Notice the fragrance of the grass,
trees, and flowers, or whatever is there. . . . Observe whether
the meadow is sloping or flat. . . . Notice the colors. . . . Feel the
warmth of the sun radiating down upon you and warming up the
whole meadow. . . . Now you walk to the edge of the meadow and
discover a wilderness or desert. Stand there for awhile and
become aware what you experience, observing that barren
area. . . . Before your eyes, let the desert bloom. . . . See it
bloom. . . . Become aware how you feel as you see the desert

bloom before you. . . . Look around and notice the colors, the fragrances, maybe the sounds. . . . Allow yourself to feel a part of this blooming. . . . With a sense of this blooming with you, reach out and pick up some gift symbol to represent this blooming desert. As you find this, make your way back to the meadow at your own pace, and in your own way. . . . When you get back to the meadow, look around and observe the meadow again. . . . If there is anything that you have not had a chance to finish, go back and do whatever you need to do. . . . Remember the gift symbol that you bring back from the wilderness or desert. When you feel ready, open your eyes.

Comments on Debriefing and Use: To draw first the meadow, then the wilderness or desert in bloom could be both very beautiful and powerful. You could ask, "What part of my life is the meadow, the wilderness, or the desert?" Notice the connections between your life and the images in the meditation.

12

Affirming Our Unity in Diversity

Reading: For Christ is like a single body with its many limbs and organs, which, many as they are, together make up one body.... A body is not one single organ, but many. Suppose the foot should say, "Because I am not a hand, I do not belong to the body," it does belong to the body none the less. Suppose the ear were to say, "Because I am not an eye, I do not belong to the body," it does still belong to the body. If the body were all eye, how could it hear? If the body were all ear, how could it smell? But, in fact, God appointed each limb and organ to its own place in the body, as he chose. If the whole were one single organ, there would not be a body at all; in fact, however, there are many different organs, but one body. The eye cannot say to the hand, "I do not need you"; nor the head to the feet, "I do not need you." ... If one organ suffers, they all suffer together. If one flourishes, they all rejoice together (1 Corinthians 12:12, 14-21, 26).

Biblical Note: Paul is saying that the church *is* the body of Christ. He is telling the people that they should honor each other because of their differences rather than simply putting up with their differences. He is seeking to create a climate of unity within diversity. He also may be reassuring those who do not speak in tongues that indeed they are vital parts of the church. We require one another, with each having different gifts. In fact, we need to experience another's joy as our own joy and another's sorrow as our own sorrow.

For Your Meditation: You may think of the *body* as your family, the community, your church, the church, or the whole community of persons. This meditation is quite long, for there is a lengthy section just to relax. You may want to omit the first part or use the first part as a relaxation exercise by itself.

Meditation: (a) Sit quietly and let yourself relax, taking a few deep breaths. . . . Now become aware of your toes and let them relax. . . . Become aware of your feet. Allow them to tense, then let them relax. . . . Focus on your calves; tense them, then relax. . . . Tet your thighs tense, then relax. . . . Feel your whole legs relaxing, letting go. . . . Relax your lower abdomen. . . . Feel your stomach tensing, then relaxing. . . . Let a large breath flow through you and feel your chest cavity relaxing. . . . Feel your upper arms tense, then relax. . . . Tense your wrists and hands and lower arms, then relax. . . . Tense your neck muscles, let them relax. . . . Let a sense of relaxation radiate from the center of your forehead throughout your face. Feel your cheek muscles relax. . . . Relax your jaw. . . . Feel your tongue relaxing, and your throat. . . . Relax your scalp. . . . Go back through your body and sense if there are any tight spots; simply let them relax. . . .

(b) Now become aware of your feet; simply focus your awareness on your feet. Move your feet and remain focused in attention on your feet. . . . Become aware of your whole body responding to the movement of your feet. Stop moving your feet, and feel your body's response. Now place your attention on your stomach. Move your stomach around from within. . . . Get a sense of your body as a whole, responding to the movement of your stomach. Continue to do this with various parts of your body, putting your attention at the one point, focusing your awareness there, then moving your attention to an awareness of your whole body. Then become aware of the flow between that part of the body and the whole body. . . .

Now reflect on your family, community, the church, the church to which you belong, or the whole world. . . . Become aware of yourself within that community. . . . Think of yourself and the role that you play in this community. . . . Consider your responsibility, your functions, your gifts. . . . Now become aware of the whole community and the flow between you and the community. Sense this flow. . . . Move your awareness to another person within this community. . . . What is that person's role and function within the community? Now sense the flow between that person and the community. . .the flow be-

76

tween that person and you within the community. Identify some joy in that other person and experience how that affects you. . . . Become aware of some joy within yourself and experience how that affects the person. . . . Reflect on some sorrow or pain within that person. . . . Now become aware of the effect of that sorrow in your experience. . . . Likewise, remember some pain in your own life. . . . Now get some sense of how that affects her/his life. . . . If there is someone else within this community on whom you wish to focus, go ahead, and again go through the interaction between the two of you. . . . Do this as long as it feels right, with as many people within the community as you choose. . . . When you feel finished, become aware of yourself, your gift to this community, your function. Consider if there is anything that you want to change. . . . Experience a sense of acceptance of yourself as you are, and as you are becoming. Now again become aware of your body in its full flow of functioning. . . . When you are ready, open your eyes.

Comments on Debriefing and Use: I would think that a family during their normal activities or on a vacation would benefit from doing this meditation together, then sharing the responses. Or, a committee meeting within a church could also benefit from this. You may discover not only other people's perception of your functions, but also a level of concern of which you had been unaware. Be sure to allow for an acceptance of whatever occurs. In other words, it is important not to judge a person's perceptions as fact but, rather, as her/his perception at that particular point in time. If a relationship is facing a challenge or simply struggling to grow, this meditation might be valuable to use in a community of two.

Each person has certain roles and functions which are important and valuable. This does not imply, however, that a person need not change if she/he becomes aware that these roles are limiting. Whether your group be a church school class, a church meeting, a family, or a pair, you might draw a diagram which represents all your gifts and functions as you see them and how you interact with each other. Then you can affirm each other and reflect upon possible changes.

13

Blessing the Child Within Us

Reading: They brought children for him to touch. The disciples rebuked them, but when Jesus saw this he was indignant, and said to them, "Let the children come to me; do not try to stop them; for the kingdom of God belongs to such as these. I tell you, whoever does not accept the kingdom of God like a child will never enter it." And he put his arms round them, laid his hands upon them, and blessed them (Mark 10:13-16; see also Matthew 19:13-15, Luke 18:15-17 for parallel versions).

Biblical Note: Adult skepticism and inertia in acting or changing were resistances which Jesus met in his ministry. He lifted up children as those filled with trust and a willingness to change and act.

For Your Meditation: The "child within" is a way of referring to that part of us which is like a child. Any number of qualities can emerge.

Meditation: Take a few deep breaths to relax deeply. . . . Now get a sense of yourself as a child at home, at the beach, a meadow, or wherever you want to go. . . . Simply discover that child within you and express that childlikeness in whatever way you wish. . . . Feel free to bring in friends if you want, or to be alone. . . . Continue as long as you choose; simply let go and be the child. . . . Now hear the Christ's words, "The kingdom of God belongs to such as these. . . ." Become aware of your response to these words. If you wish, communicate with the Christ in any way that seems appropriate for you. . . . When you finish, bid farewell, knowing that you can return. . . . Return to your present environment and sit quietly before opening your eyes.

Comments on Debriefing and Use: A good follow-up would be to act out being this child. It might be different from your meditation, but also include some of the qualities of childlikeness that were embodied in the meditation. You might draw the child within you and/or write about that child.

14
Spiritual Matters and/or Responsibilities

Reading: While they were on their way Jesus came to a village where a woman named Martha made him welcome in her home. She had a sister, Mary, who seated herself at the Lord's feet and stayed there listening to his words. Now Martha was distracted by her many tasks, so she came to him and said, "Lord, do you not care that my sister has left me to get on with the work by myself? Tell her to come and lend a hand." But the Lord answered, "Martha, Martha, you are fretting and fussing about so many things; but one thing is necessary. The part that Mary has chosen is best; and it shall not be taken away from her" (Luke 10:38-42).

Biblical Note: This passage can be understood to mean that Jesus held concern for the spiritual life to be more important than concern over food and drink. It might, too, indicate that Jesus felt that Martha was making too lavish an occasion, that simple hospitality would have been fine.

For Your Meditation: I enjoy this encounter because I experience this conflict within myself! We need to be careful not to see the role which is so often assigned to women, concern for food and drink, as denigrated. I think that we can affirm, also, that all our activities can be aimed toward growth in the spiritual life. However, this conflict between concern for "spiritual matters" and concern for what we call "chores" is within each of us—male or female. This meditation is intended to focus on that conflict as it may emerge within you.

Meditation: Become quiet, take a few deep, slow breaths, and let go of concerns or tensions. . . . Simply be quiet. . . . Now, with your eyes closed, visualize a home and see Martha, Mary, and Jesus within this home. Look around and get a true sense of what this home is like. . . . Notice that Jesus is sitting, talking, and that Mary is listening to Jesus speak. . . . Now notice that Martha is involved with many, many activities; she is getting ready for the dinner and taking care of activities around the house. . . . See her scurrying about the house taking care of these chores. . . . Now Martha comes and protests to Jesus, "Shouldn't Mary be helping me?" she says. . . . And Jesus responds, "Martha, Martha, don't worry so much about all those things. One thing is important, and what Mary has chosen is best. I would not ask her to give up the discussion that we're having." Think over this scene and allow it to become very real for you. . . . You might experience yourself being each of these three people. . . .

Now become aware of yourself as who you truly are. . . . Reflect on the Martha and Mary part of you: the part of you which seeks to grow and to take time to focus upon spiritual things and the part of you which seeks to put things in order in your home or to take care of chores and activities which seem to be so necessary. . . . Allow these two parts of you to talk to each other or to communicate in any way which they want. . . . You might invite the Christ into your communication and ask for advice or guidance. You may reach some resolution. . . . Feel free to be innovative, to do whatever you need to do. . . . When you feel ready, become aware of your surroundings, reflect upon the experience which you just had. . . . Give thanks for your added insight and open your eyes.

Comments on Debriefing and Use: Drawing Martha and Mary and the Christ, or the Martha and Mary part of you, would be fun and also produce additional insights, for it would show how the parts relate to each other. Any group of men and women within the church might follow this meditation, then share together their experiences.

15

Reflection

Reading: "I am the real vine, and my Father is the gardener. Every barren branch of mine he cuts away; and every fruiting branch he cleans, to make it more fruitful still. You have already been cleansed by the word that I spoke to you. Dwell in me, as I in you. No branch can bear fruit by itself, but only if it remains united with the vine; no more can you bear fruit, unless you remain united with me.

"I am the vine, and you the branches. He who dwells in me, as I dwell in him, bears much fruit; for apart from me you can do nothing. He who does not dwell in me is thrown away like a withered branch. The withered branches are heaped together, thrown on the fire, and burnt.

"If you dwell in me, and my words dwell in you, ask what you will, and you shall have it. This is my Father's glory, that you may bear fruit in plenty and so be my disciples. As the Father has loved me, so I have loved you. Dwell in my love. If you heed my commands, you will dwell in my love, as I have heeded my Father's commands and dwell in his love. I have spoken thus to you, so that my joy may be in you, and your joy complete" (John 15:1-11).

Biblical Note: The *vine* in the Old Testament is often used to mean "Israel," as in Psalm 80:8-19. In the Gospel of John, the Father is described as the vine-dresser. He removes the unfruitful branches; he prunes the rest. This allegory is a beautiful expression of mystical union, similar to Paul's allegory of the body and its members. The union is between the Christian and Christ, with love as the chief mark of this inner flow. There are three results of the union with Christ: (1) prayer will be more effective because one would not ask for anything that is not in accord with the will of Christ, (2) glorification will take place through the fruitfulness of character and service, (3) joy will flow from Christ to the individual.

For Your Meditation: Similar to the meditation on the seeds (number 4), this meditation offers the opportunity to reflect upon one's whole life—to affirm some parts and to let go of other parts.

Meditation: Take a few deep breaths. . . . Get a sense of yourself in some grassy area. . . . It might be a meadow or a garden. . . . Be aware of your feelings being there. . . . Look all around you to see what is there. Notice if there are any people or plants. . . . Now become aware of the grass, how high it is, the color, the fragrances. . . . Let yourself feel the warmth of the sun radiating down upon you and the whole area. Now walk until you find a vine, a beautiful vine. . . . Notice the branches, how they intertwine. . . . Notice the fruit, the blossoms, the colors. . . . Observe some of the twigs that look as though they are just about dead. . .the twigs that need to be bent off. . . . Now become aware that there is someone who is in charge of this garden, and this vine. . .a gardener. The gardener takes care of the vine, of each of the branches. . . . Stay in touch with this caring. . .and the love of the gardener. . . . Now you hear the words, "I am the real vine, and God is the gardener. Every barren branch of mine is cut away; and every fruiting branch God cleans to make it more fruitful still." Allow yourself to become aware of a barren branch. It might be something in your life or something in life as you see it which is barren. . . . Let that be trimmed away. . . . Now look for a branch that does have fruit on it, yet needs slight pruning. . . . Allow something to come to mind in your life or life as you see it which needs pruning, and let that happen. . . . You can ask for whatever help you need. . . . Now look for some very fruitful branch. . . . Let something out of your life which is fruitful come to your mind. . . . Observe that; get a sense of the life of the vine moving through that fruit. . . . If you need to go back and finish anything, do that. . . . Think back over the three things that emerged for you and experience them again. . . . Take a look at this garden. . . . Sense the warmth, the life flowing through it, the care within it. . . . Become aware of your breathing, the room in which you are sitting, and when you are ready, open your eyes.

Comments on Debriefing and Use: The potential value of drawing, or in some way sharing your experience, cannot be overstressed, especially with this meditation. This meditation lends itself well to the context of communion.

16

In Time of Trouble

Reading: From midday a darkness fell over the whole land, which lasted until three in the afternoon; and about three Jesus cried aloud, *"Eli, Eli, lema sabachthani?"*, which means, "My God, my God, why hast thou forsaken me?" (Matthew 27:45-46).

Biblical Note: It is not clear at all what Jesus meant by this statement. It is a verse from Psalm 22, and he may have been repeating various verses of the Psalms, perhaps meditating on them. However, Jesus may have been expressing a sense of loneliness or bewilderment.

For Your Meditation: In times of trouble or crisis, we say all sorts of things which both help to release us from the crisis and have meaning in themselves. This meditation is intended to be open-ended for you. It would seem natural that this meditation would be most appropriate in a time of crisis. However, the crisis may be long-term, such as a decision requiring much time and consideration, or an immediate crisis. This meditation should be used only after some practice with guided imagery meditations and only when there is ample time for sharing openly.

Meditation: Become quiet and take several slow, deep breaths, until you feel relaxed. . . . Now allow the crisis or challenge or decision to emerge before you in your imagination. . . . If you want to say something to God or to any person, go ahead and express that with as much intensity as you want. . . . If you want, you may talk with the Christ and share feelings and ideas. . . . If you need any help or assistance, you can always bring that assistance into your meditation. When you feel that you have expressed what you need to express, let yourself finish the dialogue and say good-bye. . . . You can return to this imagery whenever you choose. . . . Resolution may occur, or simply a feeling of relief. . . . When you feel ready, affirm Amen and open your eyes.

Comments on Debriefing and Use: You may want to write out the dialogue or images which occurred. If this is done in a group, be sure several people share.

The meditation is not directed toward a definite resolution because sometimes a person needs time to experience fully the crisis. Getting in touch with those deep feelings is also important. Resolution does emerge, but the timing may be a few hours or days away, perhaps not at the time of this deep feeling.

According to the situation, you may want to work toward a resolution during the debriefing by continuing a dialogue and moving into another meditation. Or you may wish to reflect on your feelings until resolution or peace emerges.

17

The Announcement of Birth Through You

Reading: The angel went in and said to her, "Greetings, most favoured one! The Lord is with you." But she was deeply troubled by what he said and wondered what this greeting might mean. Then the angel said to her, "Do not be afraid, Mary, for God has been gracious to you; you shall conceive and bear a son, and you shall give him the name Jesus" (Luke 1:28-31).

Biblical Note: This is an announcement to Mary that she will give birth, just as Zechariah received the awareness that his wife Elizabeth would give birth. *Angel* refers to a messenger from God.

For Your Meditation: Whether you are a man or a woman, you can experience birth in many ways: the birth of a project in your life; the birth of a gift to offer your family, your community, the world; the birth of an idea; the birth of a child. Allow yourself in this meditation to be open to the many meanings of birth. You may want to create a meditation based upon Zechariah (Luke 1:8-15a), for that is a good variation of this same theme. I am using *wise person* rather than an angel as the messenger in this meditation. The wise person for you may be a friend or someone whom you respect, but do not know. Or, it may be a symbol or an unknown voice. You do not need to know now what it will be; simply enter into meditation and let it appear.

Meditation: Sit quietly and relax, taking a few deep breaths. . . . Allow yourself to let go of any thoughts, tensions, or ideas. . . . Simply let go. . . . Now imagine a wise person appearing before you. This may be a person you know or an imaginary wise person. It might even be a flower or any other symbol of wisdom for you. This wise person speaks to you . . . saying, "Do not be afraid, for God has been gracious to you; you are about to give birth. . . ." Feel free to communicate with the symbol of wisdom. . . . You may want to understand more completely what this birth is. . . . If so, allow yourself to focus on this birth as long as it feels right for you. . . . If you are not clear about what is being announced, simply let yourself sense the feeling of expectancy. . . . When you feel ready, say good-bye to the wise person. Reflect on your feelings about the expected birth. . . . When you feel ready, give thanks for the potential within you and open your eyes.

Comments on Debriefing and Use: This meditation requires a period of silence afterwards, simply to let the message soak in. Because this meditation may be abstract, remember the three levels of meanings for images, discussed on pages 41-42. You may draw the wise person or the expected birth. It definitely would be helpful to write down what has been announced, so it will be clearer to you. Later you can look back and reflect upon the growth that has taken place.

You might even fill out an "Announcement of Birth," or a "Birth Certificate." If you place this announcement on a wall, it may continue to evoke the sense of birth. If this is being done in a group, a discussion might follow. The group may decide to look at the "Announcement of Birth" a month later to see what has taken place.

18

Temptations for Us

Reading: Jesus was then led away by the Spirit into the wilderness, to be tempted by the devil. For forty days and nights he fasted, and at the end of them he was famished. The tempter approached him and said, "If you are the Son of God, tell these stones to become bread." Jesus answered, "Scripture says, 'Man cannot live on bread alone; he lives on every word that God utters.'"

The devil then took him to the Holy City and set him on the parapet of the temple. "If you are the Son of God," he said, "throw yourself down; for Scripture says, 'He will put his angels in charge of you, and they will support you in their arms, for fear you should strike your foot against a stone.'" Jesus answered him, "Scripture says again, 'You are not to put the Lord your God to the test.'"

Once again, the devil took him to a very high mountain, and showed him all the kingdoms of the world in their glory. "All these," he said, "I will give you, if you will only fall down and do me homage." But Jesus said, "Begone, Satan! Scripture says, 'You shall do homage to the Lord your God and worship him alone'" (Matthew 4:1-10; see also Mark 1:12-13, Luke 4:1-13 for parallel versions).

Biblical Note: It might be a little difficult to see what the three temptations were. The first was that Jesus allow miracles to take place which would satisfy an immediate need or hunger; the second, that he convince others, and himself as well, that he was in the right vocation and that his mission was certain; and the third, that he would use miracles to obtain political power.

For Your Meditation: These three temptations are definitely still with us. We are often tempted to pray for specific needs as if we are using God to provide for us what we want. We are tempted to ask for some type of certainty in our life, some form of security which cannot be offered. Or, we are tempted to ask for security and certainty in our faith. Finally we are tempted to seek power over other people in politics or relationships, rather than recognizing our own integrity and that of others. Experience this meditation as a way to become more aware of where you are. If you are content, recognize this. If you are dissatisfied, then you can choose to change.

Meditation: Sit quietly and take a few deep breaths. . . . Now, imagine a large blank sheet of paper in front of you and see the words, "Temptation Number One." See written on that paper, "Wanting above all else to satisfy my immediate needs. . . ." See that phrase and be aware of whatever occurs for you. . . . Simply acknowledge what appears and let it be. . . . Turn the page and see on the second sheet the words, "Temptation Number Two." You see the phrase, "Wanting certainty or proof. . . ." Reflect on the feelings which emerge for you. . . . Now turn that page and see the words, "Temptation Number Three." Wait a moment, then notice the phrase, "Wanting power or control over others. . . ." Think about that phrase. . . . Now recall what has occurred for you as you considered these three temptations. . . . Call upon the Christ, or any other person, symbol, or idea which you choose and dialogue with that person, image, or idea about your feelings. . . . Allow some guidance or resolution to emerge. . . . As you discuss your experience, you might imagine going out into the sunlight to get greater warmth and light. . . . Take whatever time you need. . . . Wait for guidance and new understanding. . . . Experience being accepted by God. . . . When you feel ready, open your eyes.

Comments on Debriefing and Use: This exercise involves both a confrontation and an acceptance. It is my conviction that in this way we grow. However, it may be more helpful to share with a friend or a group what occurred for you, so that you can discuss the temptations and your relationship to God. You could draw the three sheets of paper with the accompanying insights.

90

19

Getting a Sense of Your Growth

Reading: He said, "The kingdom of God is like this. A man scatters seed on the land; he goes to bed at night and gets up in the morning, and the seed sprouts and grows—how, he does not know. The ground produces a crop by itself, first the blade, then the ear, then full-grown corn in the ear; but as soon as the crop is ripe, he plies the sickle, because harvest-time has come" (Mark 4:26-29).

Biblical Note: This is one of the three different parables about seeds. This one shows the mystery of growth. Jesus is teaching the inevitability of the coming of the kingdom of God, after the seed is sown.

For Your Meditation: You might think of a particular "seed" in your life (faith, profession, relationship, hobby, discipline); you might let this be a meditation on your life in general; or, you might think in terms of the whole kingdom of God.

Meditation: Take a few deep breaths, sitting in an upright, straight position. Be at the seaside. . . . Feel the sand below your feet, warm and supportive. . . . Feel the warmth of the sun bathing your body with its rays. . . . Look around to see what is there. . . . Notice any rocks or greenery or animals or people. . . . Now as you walk along the sand, notice a group of people farther down the beach. . . . Gradually walk up to them and observe that one seems to be teaching the others—that one is the Christ. As you mingle with the crowd, you find that Christ is handing out a seed to everyone. He says to you that the seed represents your life, or some aspect of your life, sustained and nurtured by God. . . . You receive your seed. . . . You walk away to wherever you want to go to plant your seed. . . . Let it grow and watch it unfold and mature to represent your life right now. . . . What is happening to it? What stage is it in? . . . You may want to communicate with your growing seed; it may have a message for you. Be open to whatever happens. . . . When you feel ready, let the meaning of this experience deepen and affirm it by saying Amen.

Comments on Debriefing and Use: This meditation is very helpful in developing self-awareness. Definitely you will change. It is important not to become attached to this symbol, whether you are excited by it, confronted, or disappointed. You might stay alert to magazine pictures or photos which fit your image, or draw one yourself. If a group joins in this, you could make a mural of "Our Growth."

Cleansing

Reading: "Alas for you, lawyers and Pharisees, hypocrites! You clean the outside of cup and dish, which you have filled inside by robbery and self-indulgence! Blind Pharisee! Clean the inside of the cup first; then the outside will be clean also" (Matthew 23:25-26).

Biblical Note: It was customary in Jesus' time, according to the laws of ceremonial purity, to keep water on hand to purify people's bodies and their vessels (Mark 7:2-4, John 2:6). Naturally, the rabbis were more concerned about the inside of the cup or the vessel than the outside. Jesus was comparing the external cleanliness of the vessels to the internal uncleanliness of people's hearts and minds. Perhaps he was referring to the body rather than the vessel when he referred to the external cleanliness. Jesus is arguing that the rules for holiness are a hindrance to righteousness rather than a necessity. One can easily become preoccupied with the rules and neglect the inner meaning and transformation of life that is required.

For Your Meditation: This meditation may be used before sleep at night, or at least in the evening. However, with very few changes, it could be applied to worship settings or to any other time during the day.

Meditation: Become quiet and take a few slow, deep breaths. . . . Feel that breath moving through your entire body, as you let go of tensions and feel the strength within you. . . . Now slowly look back through the day, and think of the things you have done, those things about which you feel good. . . . You may start in the morning and move through the day, affirming yourself for the acts, activities, external deeds,

and accomplishments which fit into your concept of *good*. . . .
Now, think back through the day, and reflect upon what you
might have done—a thought which you might have shared with
someone, a helpful gesture to a person, activities which you
wished you had done. And, as you think back through the day,
imagine your body becoming clean on the outside. . . . Imagine
water flowing over your body. . . . Notice whether anything else
is left that you need to observe, acknowledge, and let go. . . .
When you feel quite cleansed, turn your attention to within.

Become aware of how you felt, what you thought and experienced this day. Acknowledge those thoughts and feelings which
were constructive to life. . . . Now, recall those thoughts and
feelings which were not constructive to life, either your life or
the lives of others. . . . Imagine water pouring through the inside of your being—cleansing it. Get a sense of yourself being
clean and pure within. . . . Identify any feelings or thoughts or
experiences remaining that need to be acknowledged and
cleansed. . . . When you have done this, sit quietly for a few
minutes and let your mind be as still as possible. If any thought
emerges for you, acknowledge it and let it go. . . . Simply sit
quietly. . . . When you feel finished, open your eyes.

Comments on Debriefing and Use: It is helpful to
think back over the day and simply observe the events of the
day, in order to gain a fresh perspective. In this meditation, we
acknowledge those places we need to clean. However, we do not
need to affirm how miserable we are as we acknowledge these
"unclean" parts. We can simply acknowledge them and at the
same time make room for more cleanliness tomorrow and in the
future. Without the sense of judgment which is found in
acknowledgment, we may not identify those things which need
improvement.

An effective exercise would be to draw yourself as a vessel,
using words or symbols which represent what was cleansed
away. This whole exercise can be done with a joyful, confrontive,
and fun spirit.

21

Multiplying Guidance for Feeding the Hungry

Reading: Some time later Jesus withdrew to the farther shore of the Sea of Galilee (or Tiberias), and a large crowd of people followed who had seen the signs he performed in healing the sick. Then Jesus went up the hillside and sat down with his disciples. It was near the time of Passover, the great Jewish festival. Raising his eyes and seeing a large crowd coming towards him, Jesus said to Philip, "Where are we to buy bread to feed these people?" This he said to test him; Jesus himself knew what he meant to do. Philip replied, "Twenty pounds would not buy enough bread for every one of them to have a little." One of his disciples, Andrew, the brother of Simon Peter, said to him, "There is a boy here who has five barley loaves and two fishes; but what is that among so many?" Jesus said, "Make the people sit down." There was plenty of grass there, so the men sat down, about five thousand of them. Then Jesus took the loaves, gave thanks, and distributed them to the people as they sat there. He did the same with the fishes, and they had as much as they wanted. When everyone had had enough, he said to his disciples, "Collect the pieces left over, so that nothing may be lost." This they did, and filled twelve baskets with the pieces left uneaten of the five barley loaves (John 6:1-13, see also Mark 6:30-44, Matthew 14:13-21 for parallel versions).

Biblical Note: This is an occasion when Jesus and a large number of his followers in Galilee broke bread together. The Eucharist or Lord's Supper is usually related to the last meal of Jesus with his twelve disciples. However, many common meals are described in the Gospels which have a distinctively religious character. Eating and drinking is frequently seen to be connected with the satisfaction of spiritual needs. Notice that Jesus gave thanks. The usual prayer at the beginning of a

Jewish meal is "Blessed art thou, O Lord our God, King of the world, who has brought forth bread from the earth."

Barley bread was the common food of the poor people. Fish was a delicacy which was eaten as a relish with the bread. In early Christian art, the bread and fish are used as symbols of the Eucharist.

For Your Meditation: You might think of hunger in the literal sense, expressing concern for the world hunger situation. Or, you might think of hunger in the metaphorical sense, focusing upon spiritual or intellectual hunger, or the hunger for meaning.

Meditation: Take three deep breaths. . . . Get a sense of yourself walking along a somewhat deserted beach. . . . Become aware of how hard or soft the sand is below your feet. Notice whether there are any other people—or any other forms of life. . . . Sense the fragrance of this beach. . . . Observe the colors of the water and sand. . . . It is a warm and sunny day. Feel that warmth moving through your body. . . . Now become aware that you are holding a picnic basket. As you walk along the beach, you notice a figure at the top of a small hill. . . . You look and see as you get closer that the figure is the Christ. . . . You climb up this small hill and greet the Christ. Greet each other and communicate in whatever way is right for you. . . . Identify the qualities which you experience. . . . As you sit or stand, talking with each other, the Christ asks you what you have in your picnic basket. . . . You open it and present what is there. As you talk about the food, it occurs to you that there are many people around the world who are hungry. You ask how these people are to be fed and wait for some answer. . . . Allow some guidance to occur. . . . See what your responsibility is. . . . If nothing precise occurs, remain open to guidance. . . . If you want to, go ahead and eat the bread or picnic lunch beside the beach. . . . Now it is time to say good-bye. . . . Become aware how you feel as you start down the hill and bid farewell to the Christ. . . . Continue to walk down to the beach. Reflect upon this event. . . . If some

96

guidance occurred, reaffirm that and any action which it may require. When you are ready, open your eyes.

Comments on Debriefing and Use: This could be used in a variety of ways: an all-church hunger dinner, grace before a family meal, thoughts before eating alone.

22

Finding and Reclaiming a Loss

Reading: "Or again, if a woman has ten silver pieces and loses one of them, does she not light the lamp, sweep out the house, and look in every corner till she has found it? And when she has, she calls her friends and neighbours together, and says, 'Rejoice with me! I have found the piece that I lost.' In the same way, I tell you, there is joy among the angels of God over one sinner who repents" (Luke 15:8-10).

Biblical Note: This parable is inserted between the parable of the lost sheep and the parable of the prodigal son in the Gospel of Luke. All three parables show how God rejoices at the renewed relationship with a person who has been lost. It is interesting that in this parable Jesus makes the analogue to God a woman. Ten coins could have been a life savings for a poor woman in Palestine at that time. The Palestinian homes were poorly provided with windows, so a lamp would likely have been necessary in order to search for the coins.

For Your Meditation: The valuables in this meditation may be possessions, ideas and/or beliefs, relationships, activities, or even memories. You may be able actually to find one of these which has been lost; however, some of these can be recovered only in a changed state. Do not be concerned that you must find it; simply stay aware to what is occurring in your imagery.

Meditation: Take three or more slow, deep breaths. Allow yourself to feel calm, centered, and relaxed. . . . Now experience yourself within a home. Look around and notice what kind of home it is, how it is decorated, where the windows are, what furniture is present, what colors and fragrances and sounds are in this home. . . . Now walk over to where you keep your valuables and look at them. . . . You realize you have lost something which is worth a great deal to you. . . . Become aware of how you feel as you discover the loss. . . .Stand there and simply experience this loss. . . . Now you begin to search for this. If you would like to turn on a light, or get a lamp, or use a flashlight, then go ahead and do that. . . . Now search all over, wherever you need to look. . . . How do you feel as you search? . . . You find it! Or you find it in some form. It may have changed. . . . Stay aware of what you experience. . . . Go back to where the rest of your valuables are. . . . Note how you feel now that you have found what you lost. . . . If it has changed, sense your feelings about that change. . . . If you want to, call a friend or neighbor and explain what has happened and share your thoughts and feelings.

Now focus upon your relationship to God. Experience whether you feel at all "lost." If so, take whatever time you need to let yourself be "found" by God. . . . Imagine God's rejoicing.

Think back over both the experience of finding something and the experience of being found. Sit in silence until you are ready, then open your eyes.

Comments on Debriefing and Use: It would be wise to write down your experience. You can also draw the house, the valuable, or your facial expressions, as you recall them from the meditation. Look again at the three levels of meaning (page 41).

23
Letting Go of Anxiety–
Accepting God's Provisions

Reading: "Therefore I bid you put away anxious thoughts about food and drink to keep you alive, and clothes to cover your body. . . . Consider how the lilies grow in the fields; they do not work, they do not spin; and yet, I tell you, even Solomon in all his splendour was not attired like one of these. . . . Set your mind on God's kingdom and his justice before everything else, and all the rest will come to you as well. So do not be anxious about tomorrow; tomorrow will look after itself. Each day has troubles enough of its own" (Matthew 6:25a, 28b-29, 33-34; see also Luke 12:22-31 for parallel version).

Biblical Note: The main thrust of this message is that we should not be distracted by cares. God has given us life. Life is a much more inclusive gift than food, so certainly God will provide food and clothing, too. This is a definite belief, not simply an encouragement offered to the people. The lilies could be any of a number of wild flowers. It has been suggested that the scarlet anemone was compared to the robes of Solomon. The teaching and metaphor used here has many roots in Jewish writings.

For Your Meditation: In our culture it is easier to feel that we are being provided for than it might be in many places around the world. For, indeed, there is starvation, malnourishment, and poverty in many forms. We can focus upon the givingness of God, both in life and in sustenance. We can also focus upon the need for human love to distribute these gifts of sustenance more fairly and equally. We can enter into this meditation if we are especially concerned about our own provisions, or about the whole human condition.

Meditation: Take three deep breaths and relax as you exhale, letting go of tensions and anxieties. . . . When you are still, visualize a flower in front of you. Observe this flower very carefully to notice the colors, fragrance, texture. . . beauty. . . . Notice this flower in as much detail as you can. . . . Now become aware of the life flowing through this flower. Think of the nutrients and the water in the soil which are nourishing the flower. . . . Sense the harmony between this flower, its environment, and the larger environment. . . .

Now become aware of yourself. Pay attention to your body and notice any part that seems tense. . . . Reflect on your emotions and any concerns you may be experiencing. . . . Pay attention to your thoughts. . . .Let these tensions, concerns, and thoughts go as you experience your rootedness in life. . . .Sense the flowing of God's life through you. . . . Compare yourself to this flower in front of you, being provided for. . . . Visualize yourself being clothed adequately. . . . Identify any resistance that you meet in visualizing this for yourself. Experience that life flowing through you again and see if it can push through that resistance. . . . Visualize yourself having enough food. If there are any resistances or doubts, become aware of them. Again, get in touch with life flowing through you and allow it to dissolve the resistances.

As you experience the life providing for the flower and for you, extend your consciousness to include all persons throughout the world. Think of the many people and living things throughout the world. . . . Become aware of the soil beneath all living things and the nurturing, giving quality of life. . . . Note any resistance, hunger, or concern. . . . Reflect on the harmony that can take place as more and more people are provided for. Stay in touch with this until you truly get a sense that this is so. . . . Again, affirm with gratitude the life providing for the flower, for you, and for all people. . . . Amen.

Comments on Debriefing and Use: This meditation can obviously be used in a time of crisis when a family is uncertain about provision for basic needs. An individual may stop in the process of paying bills and do this meditation. I feel cautious that we stay in touch with the sense that God provides, yet also not expect God to be some sort of magician who brings to us whatever we may want. If we stay alert to God's givingness to ALL and to the simple necessities of the flower, we may not expect that an enormous number of things ought naturally to flow in our particular direction. This meditation could also be used at a church function which emphasizes world concerns, world hunger, environment, or justice in the community.

24

Finding the Ground of Meaning In Your Life

Reading: "Here is another picture of the kingdom of Heaven. A merchant looking out for fine pearls found one of very special value; so he went and sold everything he had, and bought it" (Matthew 13:45-46).

Biblical Note: Merchants in search of fine pearls were likely to travel far distances, perhaps to the Persian Gulf or even to India. So, the search was often long and intense.

For Your Meditation: Kahil Gibran wrote of the pearl: "A pearl is a temple built by pain around a grain of sand. What longing built our bodies and around what grains?"[26]

Meditation: Close your eyes; sit straight and comfortably. Take three slow, deep breaths to relax. . . . Now imagine yourself in a meadow or grassy area. . . . Feel the warmth of the sun moving through your entire being. . . . Look around and see what is there with you. . . . Notice the colors of the grass and foliage, if there is any. . . . Walk around a bit to get a sense of where you are. . . .Now you notice a path . . . and another path . . . and still another path. All the paths are gentle uphill slopes. . . . You become aware that you are searching for something of great value. . . . Following your intuition and God's guidance, choose your path and do whatever is necessary in order to find that for which you are searching. . . . Let yourself experience any struggles or barriers along the way. . . . Also, bring in any help or assistance that you want. . . .Finally you find this thing of great value for which you have been searching. . . . Observe closely what this is. . . . You discover that you must sell or get rid of everything else in your life if you are to obtain this one thing. . . . Become aware of your inner experience as you make this discovery. . . . If you do decide to let go of everything else, follow through with that exchange and go back down the path to the meadow, aware of your feelings. . . .If you decide not to make the exchange, then you go on back down the path to the meadow, becoming aware how you feel about your decision. . . .Let yourself stay in the meadow for a while. . . .When you feel ready, open your eyes.

Comments on Debriefing and Use: This may be a beautiful discovery as to what is of greatest value for you. This insight can help guide you. If it has been frustrating and you could not decide, then let yourself reflect on that discovery. As a project, you might list pearls of different values, from the greatest value to the smallest. Children might enjoy making a string of pearls in church school.

25

Let Thy Glory Shine Over All the Earth

Reading: My heart is steadfast, O God,
      my heart is steadfast.
    I will sing and raise a psalm;
      awake, my spirit,
    awake, lute and harp,
      I will awake at dawn of day.
    I will confess thee, O Lord, among the peoples,
      among the nations I will raise a psalm to
      thee,
    for the unfailing love is wide as the heavens
      and thy truth reaches to the skies.
    Show thyself, O God, high above the heavens;
      let thy glory shine over all the earth (Psalm
      57:7-11).

Biblical Note: The poet of this psalm expresses enormous relief, for the turmoil of his soul has passed. He expresses a theme which is found in much of Israel's poetry: ill fortune neither ruins one's faith in God, nor does good fortune make that prior ill fortune meaningless. One both cries and sings to God out of one's depths. A moment ago the psalmist was in despair; at this point the psalmist sings with joy, strength, and faith.

For Your Meditation: Light is often identified with God. Light is identified, too, with guidance, intuition, and warmth. You may choose to do this meditation in the morning upon awakening.

Meditation: Sit quietly and allow yourself to sense a feeling of peace. Take a few deep breaths. . . . Visualize a morning horizon. . . . Notice your surroundings as you are observing this horizon. Become aware of the dawn. Allow the sun to move

slowly upward to make a very clear dawning upon the earth. . . .
Notice the warmth upon the earth increases as the sun radiates
upon it. Become aware of the darkness fading and the light
increasing as the sun dawns more fully. . . . Allow yourself to
have the magical ability to move around the whole earth and to
experience this dawn as it continues to take place. . . . Constantly experience this dawn until you have revolved around
the entire earth, returning to where you began. Stay in touch
with the radiance and warmth and light of this dawning.

Now become aware of anything or any part of the earth which
needs some light. . . . Sense the movement toward light, toward
wholeness, toward harmony. Follow through with as many dark
places as you choose. . . . Experience that radiance moving
through you and your radiating this presence out to the
world—the reciprocal giving and taking of light. . . . Settle
down to rest in the place you began. . . . Be silent for a while. . . .
When you are ready, open your eyes.

Comments on Debriefing and Use: In meditation we can
be intentionally optimistic, assuming that it is in accord with
God's will that people move toward light. You might find it
exciting to draw a large mural with the various drawings. You
can expand this meditation to include outer space, too! This can
be modified to focus upon a specific world issue. Also it can be
changed into a more private meditation by imagining the dawning to encompass one's daily activities.

26

Reconciliation

Reading: Jacob raised his eyes and saw Esau coming towards him with four hundred men. . . . He then went on ahead of them, bowing low to the ground seven times as he approached his brother. Esau ran to meet him and embraced him; he threw his arms round him and kissed him, and they wept. . . . Esau said, "What was all that company of yours that I met?" And he [Jacob] answered, "It was meant to win favour with you, my lord." Esau answered, "I have more than enough. Keep what is yours, my brother." But Jacob said, "On no account: if I have won your favour, then, I pray, accept this gift from me. . . . Accept this gift which I bring you; for God has been gracious to me, and I have all I want." So he urged him, and he [Esau] accepted it. . . . Esau said, "Let me detail some of my own men to escort you," but he [Jacob] replied, "Why should my lord be so kind to me?" (Genesis 33:1a, 3-4, 8-10, 11, 15).

Biblical Note: Twenty years prior to this meeting, Jacob had deceptively obtained Esau's birthright, received the blessing from Isaac their father, then fled from Esau. At this point the two brothers are meeting again and embracing each other in reconciliation. Jacob has just wrestled with God during the night before this meeting and has won "power with God," even to be given his new name, Israel. But he remains somewhat skeptical of Esau's open exchange of brotherly love and lack of concern for the gifts Jacob has brought. Jacob expects Esau to hold a grudge for the wrongs done to him, but Esau had dismissed his anger long ago.

For Your Meditation: You may choose to focus upon a brother or sister if you have any sense of estrangement in your relationship. Or, you may choose to focus upon any person from whom you feel separated. A humorous meditation based on the theme of reconciliation can be created with the passage from Luke 6:41-42 which refers to the speck in the other's eye and the plank in one's own.

Meditation: Become centered and quiet as you take a few deep breaths. Let go of any tensions or concerns or thoughts. . . . Imagine yourself to be in a field. Let yourself be there for a while, noticing in detail what it is like. . . . Notice if anyone is with you, or if you are alone. . . . Now visualize a person coming toward you. As this person comes closer to you, you will see that it is an individual from whom you feel estranged. . . . Notice that this person is running toward you, eager to make reconciliation, to greet you anew. . . . Be very aware of your emotions. . . . Begin to move toward this person and note how you are moving. . . . Greet this person, perhaps embrace. Allow whatever needs to take place to occur between the two of you. You may be silent together or you may talk. . . . When you are ready, observe that this person has brought with him or her a gift for you. . . . That person offers you this gift. . . . Become aware how you feel accepting it. . . . See what this person has offered to you. . . . Share with this person your response to receiving the gift. . . . Now, hold out a gift which you have brought him or her. Present this gift and permit that person to make a response to you. . . . Again, allow whatever exchange needs to take place to occur between the two of you. . . . See whether you can move on together in a sense of reconciliation, forgiveness, acceptance, and love. . . . If not, become aware what barriers prevent this. . . . Remain silent for a while, then open your eyes.

Comments on Debriefing and Use: You might, after experiencing this meditation, actually follow through and make reconciliation, or discuss the barriers with this person through a letter, call, or in person. If the person has died or is no longer available for physical contact, you may find this meditation can enable you to carry on the conversation even though the person is not near. You may want to do this meditation a number of times with the same person or various people. The gift is a beautiful way to acknowledge your love for each other in a symbolic gesture. You may draw a picture or share verbally with that person your feelings in receiving his/her gift and in giving your gift.

27

Emptying

Reading: Jesus said: The Kingdom of the [Father] is like a woman who was carrying a jar full of meal. While she was walking [on a] distant road, the handle of the jar broke. The meal streamed out behind her on the road. She did not know [it], she had noticed no accident. After she came into her house, she put the jar down, she found it empty (Gospel of Thomas 97:7-14).

Biblical Note: This parable is found nestled in other parables in the Gospel of Thomas which describe the kingdom of God. (See footnote 24 for background information on this Gospel.)

For Your Meditation: The concept of emptiness is important. It is especially so in our time, for we are realizing the importance of seeking growth in areas of potential rather than depending exclusively upon the limited natural resources. It is somewhat frightening at times to meditate upon emptiness, although there has been much of that in the Christian tradition. Yet, often the times we let go of attachments become times for appreciating anew what is of value.

Meditation: Take a few slow, deep breaths and relax. . . . Let go of any tensions or concerns and just sit. . . . Now imagine yourself to be on a road, at a distance from your home. . . . You are going to head toward home, and you reach down to pick up a heavy jar. . . . As you look at it, become aware of what is in the jar. Let it be filled with items of your life now. . . .. Now walk home, carrying the jar. . . . Observe what you pass along the way and what kind of road it is. . . . Now you are home. . . . You enter into the doorway, and you notice that the jar you have carried all the way is empty. Become aware of your feelings as you see the empty jar. . . . Now hear the words, "The kingdom of

God is like this. . . ." Let yourself experience whatever you feel or think. . . . You may want to talk with the Christ about this. . . . If you want to, bring the Christ or any person you choose into your home to talk. . . . Notice what the jar is like now. . . . Do you feel any differently now than when you first noticed it was empty? . . . Bid farewell to the person with whom you were talking, knowing you can communicate again later. . . . Sit quietly, aware of your feelings. . . . When you are ready, open your eyes.

Comments on Debriefing and Use: Sometimes it becomes clear in this meditation that there are things in our life which either we do not want or to which we are too attached. If either feeling occurs, be sure to affirm that this is only one meditation, with *one* awareness for the present time. It would be essential to reflect a great deal more before instantly letting go, unless it becomes increasingly clear that this is indicated. Sometimes nothing will occur which needs to be released. Some people find that their jars remain empty; others refill their jars in the meditation. Still others put different things back into the jar. How people feel about those occurrences vary.

You could draw the jar as it was full and as it was empty. You might draw your home and the path to see how you depict those. If the attachments involve other people, it might be wise to share your feelings with them.

28

Follow the Star to Observe Birth

Reading: They set out at the king's [Herod's] bidding; and the star which they had seen at its rising went ahead of them until it stopped above the place where the child lay. At the sight of the star they were overjoyed. Entering the house, they saw the child with Mary his mother, and bowed to the ground in homage to him; then they opened their treasures and offered him gifts: gold, frankincense, and myrrh (Matthew 2:9-12).

Biblical Note: The troubled King Herod instructed the wise men, the astrologers of the time, to search for the young child who was born in Bethlehem. The wise men's gifts were appropriate for a monarch of that time. Gold and fragrant resins were used in worship and for perfume, medicine, and embalming. After presenting the gifts, the wise men received guidance through a dream or an oracle that they should not return to Herod, but rather go to their own country via another route.

For Your Meditation: The star, diamond, sun, or source of light is very often a symbol for the higher self, guidance, or God. In this meditation, the "star" will be in line with this symbolism. The gift that the wise men brought will be symbolized for you through whatever gift you create to bring on your journey.

Meditation: Take a few slow, deep breaths and let yourself relax and let go. . . . Now get a sense of yourself walking along a grassy meadow or plains region. . . . Feel the warmth of the sun on a clear day. . . . Observe whether people are walking with you, or whether you are walking alone. . . . Watch the sun slowly setting and the sky slowly getting dark. . . . Now look at the dark night sky and a bright star. . . . Turn and follow that star, aware of your feelings and thoughts and emotions as you walk toward that star. . . . Become aware that something is going to give birth beneath that star, something of great value. . . . You are holding some gifts which you can offer. Look at these gifts that you are carrying with you. . . . Now you see ahead a setting which is indeed below this star. . . . Walk slowly up to this spot and let take place whatever occurs for you. . . . Become aware that the Christ is being born. Talk with anyone whom you choose in the scene. . . . Offer your gifts and allow an exchange to take place. . . . Stay in this setting, experiencing the power of this birth event and reflecting on the presence of the guidance of that star. . . . Finish whatever you need to finish. . . . Now say good-bye and move on, still aware of the events which took place and your experience. . . . Become aware of yourself and your surroundings. . . . When you feel ready, open your eyes.

Comments on Debriefing and Use: This would be a good meditation to do in a church school or worship service at Christmas. Children might like to create the gift they brought and to illustrate the birth event which is taking place. You might reflect upon how this birth occurs in your life.

29

Meditation Upon Saying Good-bye

Reading: "Set your troubled hearts at rest. Trust in God always; trust also in me. There are many dwelling-places in my Father's house; if it were not so I should have told you; for I am going there on purpose to prepare a place for you!" (John 14:1-2).

Biblical Note: Whereas the words *dwelling-places* are used in this version, *mansions* is found in the King James Version, and *rooms* is used in the Revised Standard Version. Jesus is comforting his disciples and himself, for they have been troubled by the thought of the impending betrayal, separation, and death. Jesus says that they should have faith, believing in God and in him.

For Your Meditation: You might enter into this meditation with someone in mind who died several years ago and for whom you still grieve. Or you may have in mind a person who is leaving, or whom you are leaving, so that your relationship is pulling apart physically. Perhaps you may have in mind somebody who is dying, and you want to stay in touch with the strength and faith that Jesus taught. I recommend this meditation only for those who have already practiced others. Also, if this is practiced in a group, each person should have time to share.

Meditation: Become quiet and take three slow, deep breaths as you relax and let go of any thoughts or tensions or concerns. . . . Now become aware of yourself walking in a meadow. Observe the grass, its color, fragrance. . . . Notice what flowers, trees, or foliage are in the meadow. . . . See that it is a warm, bright, sunny day, and feel that warmth moving through your own body. . . . Notice if there is anyone with you there in the meadow, or if you are there alone. . . . Now begin to walk along a gently sloping path, sloping upward away from the meadow. Walk along that path. . . . Observe carefully the path, how you are walking, and what is along the pathway. . . . Now you come to a dwelling. As you walk up to that dwelling, you see written across the front doorway, "In God's House There Are Many Dwelling Places." You stand there and notice the outside of this house. . . . When you feel ready, walk into this house. . . . When you have looked at the various rooms, walk into whatever room you choose. . . . Pay attention to your whole experience while you are in this room. . . . Notice how you feel, your attitude toward the room, the details of the room. . . . Now see who dwells in this room. . . . This is someone to whom you either have said good-bye or are saying good-bye, and for whom you affirm that there is a dwelling. . . . Allow that person to be there now in this room. Interact with this person in any way that you wish, for as long as you want. . . . Now ask this person for some token—maybe a few words or a gift—which he/she can give to you to keep. . . . Watch how this person offers this gift and how you receive it. If you choose to give a gift to this person, go ahead and do that. . . . Now say good-bye in any way that feels right for you. . . . Go back to the center near the front doorway and observe if there is any other room where you wish to go. If there is, go through the same process of observing the room, interacting with the person who lives there, asking for and sharing a gift, and leaving. . . . When you feel ready, go back to the front door and say good-bye to the whole house. . . . Think back through the rooms which you have visited and think back on the people and the gifts shared. . . . Now walk out of the house, and walk on back to the meadow. . . . In the meadow notice what you are doing with the gift or gifts that you have. . . . Allow yourself to feel again the warmth of the sun on this day. . . . Become aware of your surroundings where you are sitting and your body. When you are ready, open your eyes.

Comments on Debriefing and Use: This meditation was used at a funeral service and was quite moving, for it gave people the chance to say good-bye to the person who had died.

Sometimes we want to carry on dialogues with a person who has just died, and occasionally we are not sure whether it is "right" somehow to do this. A meditation like this gives "permission" for this dialogue process. I would use it only as it seems appropriate in these circumstances.

This meditation certainly does not need to be about people who have died or are dying, but also can be about people, places, or things to which you need to say good-bye, either because you are moving or there is a change in your conditions. In our fast-changing world, these "good-byes" are often!

Drawings or small constructions of any kind would be possible follow-ups for this. For many children, this would be a valuable experience before moving and saying good-bye to playmates at school. It is also helpful in some divorce situations.

Bidding Good-bye and Blessings

Reading: And now, my friends, farewell. Mend your ways; take our appeal to heart; agree with one another; live in peace; and the God of love and peace will be with you. Greet one another with the kiss of peace. All God's people send you greetings. The grace of the Lord Jesus Christ, and the love of God, and fellowship in the Holy Spirit, be with you all (2 Corinthians 13:11-14).

Biblical Note: This is the last bit of Paul's second letter to the church at Corinth. The word *farewell* may also mean "rejoice." If the translation is *farewell,* then it means more clearly, "may things go well with you." "Mend your ways" is Paul's way of urging them to work towards perfection, or continue in the process. "Heed my appeal" may mean "be exorted" or, possibly, "keep encouraging one another." "Be of one mind" is a warning against the divisiveness that was going on in Corinth at the time. In the early church, the exchanging of the holy kiss of peace was a common phenomenon. It was called *holy* because all people within the church are considered saints, and the kiss between saints would then be a holy kiss. The grace of the Lord Jesus Christ is the free gift of Christ opening the way both to faith and new life. The love of God is an act of reaching out by God. The last three words, "with you all," imply that Paul had no leftover grudges or unfinished business with the members of the church at Corinth, even though they had caused a great many trials and problems for him.

For Your Meditation: If you are using this meditation at the beginning of a group gathering or worship service or family get-together, then you may substitute the word *rejoice* for *farewell.* This meditation is written with the idea of a small group in mind, whether that be a family or growth group setting. If you are doing this as a large group, simply alter it by having people say good-bye to some people, not every person. This is the least concrete meditation of this book. It would be best to have experienced some of the ones which are easier to image prior to doing this.

Meditation: Become quiet and take a few, slow, deep breaths. . . . You hear the words, "And now, my friends, farewell! Mend your ways: take our appeal to heart; agree with one another. . . ." Get a sense of each person, the whole group, continuing to grow. Think of us all going out and continuing in this path toward growth that we have shared together. . . . Reflect on the various people here and affirm that growth and positive changes are taking place in the way that we live. . . . You hear the words, "May you live in peace." Share peace with each person here. . . . Extend this sense of peace to include the broader world. . . . Experience each of us radiating peace as we go forth. . . . You hear, "The God of love and peace will be with you. Greet one another with the kiss of peace." Get a sense of greeting each other with a kiss of peace. Then greet the people around you in your imagination right now and give blessings to each. . . . If you want to say something or communicate in some way, go ahead. . . . Again, you hear "The grace of the Lord Jesus Christ. . . ." Experience the grace of the Lord Jesus Christ being present within this group and within each one. . . . Get in touch with this grace as freely given love. . . . If any images emerge, become aware of what they are. . . . Finally, you hear, "And the love of God. . . ." Discover a sense of the love of God in our midst, within this group, and within each one. . . ." And fellowship in the Holy Spirit, be with you all. . . ." Now reflect on the fellowship of the Holy Spirit, however you experience this within this group. . . . Expand your consciousness to reach out as far as you can, or as far as you want to, to greet all people with the kiss of peace, to experience the grace of the Lord, the love of God, and the fellowship of the Holy Spirit. Let us affirm together, "Amen."

Comments on Debriefing and Use: This meditation could be shortened and made less complicated by ending with the image of the kiss of peace rather than including the benediction (which begins with "the grace of the Lord Jesus Christ"). Each person within the group may wish to share his/her experience, and then the group can decide how to close. This meditation does not normally lend itself easily to drawing; however if a strong image occurs, that would be appropriate. This does generally take some time to debrief; therefore, it could be the whole activity on the last night of a group.

And now, my friends, farewell.
Peace be with you.

NOTES

1. Martha Crampton, *An Historical Survey of Mental Imagery Techniques in Psychotherapy and Description of the Dialogic Imaginal Integration Method* (Montreal, Quebec: The Quebec Center for Psychosynthesis, Inc., 1974), pp. 1-2.
2. Crampton, *An Historical Survey of Mental Imagery Techniques,* pp. 2-3.
3. Crampton, *An Historical Survey of Mental Imagery Techniques,* p. 8.
4. For an excellent detailed historical survey of the therapeutic use of guided mental imagery, see Martha Crampton's book cited above.
5. Dr. Carl Simonton is a radiation therapist in private practice and Associate Director, Oncology Associates, Fort Worth. He initiated study to explore the role that the will of the patient has in successful treatment of disease and developed a new approach to cancer treatment, combining traditional treatment methods with biofeedback, meditation techniques, hypnotherapy and psychiatry, first implemented at Travis Air Force Base when he was Chief of Radiation Therapy Service.
6. Anthony Mottola, trans., *The Spiritual Exercises of St. Ignatius* (Garden City, New York: Image Books, A Division of Doubleday and Company, Inc., 1964), pp. 70-71.
7. Robert E. Ornstein, *The Psychology of Consciousness* (New York: Penguin Books by arrangement with The Viking Press, 1972), pp. 66-68, 155-157.
8. Ornstein, *The Psychology of Consciousness* and Claudio Naranjo and Robert E. Ornstein, *On the Psychology of Meditation* (New York: Viking Press, 1974).
9. John E. Biersdorf, *Hunger for Experience: Vital Religious Communities in America* (New York: The Seabury Press, Inc., 1975), pp. 24-27.
10. Biersdorf, *Hunger for Experience,* p. 21.
11. Biersdorf, *Hunger for Experience,* p. 23.
12. John B. Cobb, Jr., "The Identity of Christian Spirituality and Global Consciousness," an unpublished paper written for the faculty of the School of Theology at Claremont, Calif., Fall, 1975, pp. 1-2.
13. John B. Cobb, Jr., "Strengthening the Spirit," *Union Seminary Quarterly Review* XXX (Winter-Summer, 1975): 133.
14. John B. Cobb, Jr., "Strengthening the Spirit," p. 136.
15. John B. Cobb, Jr., "Strengthening the Spirit," p. 135.

16. Joseph Campbell, notes from a workshop given at Esalen, May 14-16, 1976, entitled, "Initiations: The Psychology of Symbolic Forms."

17. Morton T. Kelsey, *God, Dreams, and Revelation: A Christian Interpretation of Dreams* (Minneapolis: Augsburg, 1974), p. 72.

18. Mike Samuels and Hal Bennett, *The Well Body Book* (New York: Random House, 1973), and Anne Kent Rush, *Getting Clear: Body Work for Women* (New York: Random House, 1973).

19. Philip Kapleau, ed. *The Three Pillars of Zen: Teaching, Practice, and Enlightenment* (Boston: Beacon Press, 1967). See pages 315-320 for sitting postures.

20. Herbert Benson, *The Relaxation Response* (New York: William Morrow and Company, Inc., 1975).

21. Patricia Garfield, *Creative Dreaming* (New York: Simon and Schuster, 1974), pp. 101-142.

22. Ann Faraday, *The Dream Game* (New York: Harper and Row, Publishers, 1974), pp. 138-141.

23. *The New English Bible* (Oxford: Oxford University Press, 1970).

24. A. Guillaumont, H.-Ch. Puech, G. Quispel, W. Till, and Yassah 'Abd Al Masih, trans., *The Gospel According to Thomas* (New York and Evanston: Harper and Row—Leiden E. J. Brill, 1959).

The Gospel According to Thomas was discovered in 1945 in the remains of a Coptic Library in a ruined tomb near Nag Hamadi, Upper Egypt. This document contains the sayings of Jesus, many resembling those of the New Testament, but some which had never been seen before. The text must have been produced in Greek about 140 A.D.

25. *The Interpreter's Bible* (New York and Nashville: Abingdon Press, 1956, Vols. 1, 2, 4, 5, 7, 8, 10).

26. Kahil Gibran, *Sand and Foam: A Book of Aphorisms* (New York: Alfred A. Knopf, 1954), p. 4.

SUGGESTED READINGS

These suggestions are categorized into four areas which relate to the text of this book: guided imagery, dream work, meditation, and journal keeping. There are a number of books on meditation and dreams, so in these areas I have been rather selective. I have listed most of the books about journal keeping and guided imagery of which I am aware.

GUIDED IMAGERY

Andersen, Marianne, and Savary, Louis M. *Passages: A Guide for Pilgrims of the Mind.* New York: Harper and Row, 1972. This book does offer a "road map" toward expanding the mind, as is its purpose. However, the map may not be the one for you at this time. If you do not follow the road map it suggests, the quotes and theory are of value.

Assagioli, Roberto. *Psychosynthesis: A Manual of Principles and Techniques.* New York: The Viking Press, 1971. Psychosynthesis is the name of a therapeutic school which uses much guided imagery and meditation as part of individual and group growth work. This is the best total sourcebook on the topic.

Crampton, Martha. *An Historical Survey of Mental Imagery Techniques in Psychotherapy and Description of the Dialogic Imaginal Integration Method.* Montreal, Quebec: The Quebec Center for Psychosynthesis, Inc., 1974. This book is a scholarly summary of guided imagery as a tool in therapy. Following primarily the Psychosynthesis style, Crampton provides twelve transcripts from therapy sessions with commentary.

Available through High Point Foundation, Pasadena, California.

Kimmel, Jo. *Steps to Prayer Power*. Nashville: Abingdon, 1972. This is simple, almost folksy, and personal. She offers about 23 examples of meditations, most of which use visualization. She bases many of her meditations on encounters with Jesus. Sometimes they are too guided for my preference.

Masters, Robert, and Houston, Jean. *Mind Games: The Guide to Inner Space*. New York: Dell Pub. Co., 1972. I recommend this only for groups with a well-experienced leader.

Samuels, Mike, and Bennett, Hal. *The Well Body Book*. New York: Random House Inc. and Berkeley, California: The Bookworks, 1973. There is a section on visualization exercises, including creating your own imaginary doctor to help guide you. Also, there are sections on relaxation and on dreams. Throughout the book, use is made of imagery for preventative and healing medicine. This is a good resource to have at home.

Samuels, Mike, and Samuels, Nancy. *Seeing with the Mind's Eye: The History, Techniques and Uses of Visualization*. New York and Berkeley: Random House, Bookworks, 1975. Incredible resource! As the subtitle indicates, it provides a history of images and the use of visualization from many cultures. There are practical guides for relaxation and visualization connected with medicine, psychology, parapsychology, and spiritual life. There are many dramatic photographs.

Stevens, John O. *Awareness: exploring, experimenting, experiencing*. Utah: Real People Press, 1971. This is a good sourcebook with exercises for awareness, communication, "fantasy journeys," and even art and movement.

Synthesis. Redwood City, California (Journal). This offers practical guides and articles on imagination, visualization, journal keeping, meditation, and psychology, using the approach of Psychosynthesis.

JOURNAL KEEPING

Progoff, Ira. *At a Journal Workshop: The Basic Text and Guide for Using the Intensive Journal.* New York: Dialogue House, 1975. This is a highly detailed book for one who is interested in keeping a detailed journal! Even if you do not organize your journal in the precise fashion suggested, there are many good ideas for use of a journal.

Simons, George F. *Journal for Life: Discovering Faith and Values Through Journal Keeping.* Part 1: Foundations. (Other parts are due to be published.) Life in Christ, Division of ACTA, Foundation for Adult Catechetical Teaching Aids, 201 E. Ohio Street, Chicago, Illinois 60611. This booklet offers several excellent suggestions for journal keeping and group exercises. It would be valuable to use in a church setting, but would certainly not be limited to that setting.

DREAM WORK

Faraday, Ann. *The Dream Game.* New York: Harper and Row, 1974. Superb! This offers much guidance for those who want to work on their own dreams. She is well versed in the ideas of Freud, Jung, Cayce, and gestalt therapy with respect to their use of dreams. She is slightly biased, it seems, in her views of religion. When I suggest only one book for dream work, it is this one.

Faraday, Ann. *Dream Power.* New York: Coward, McCann and Geoghegan, 1972; Berkeley Medallion Books, 1973. This is fine, more informational than the above in terms of theory and less practical for the individual in my opinion.

Jung, Carl G. *Man and His Symbols.* London: Alders Books, 1964; New York: Dell, 1968. Part one offers a good introduction to Jung's valuing of dreams and dream symbols.

Jung, Carl G. *Memories, Dreams, Reflections.* New York: Random House, 1961; Vintage Books, 1962. This autobiographical statement shows the importance of dreams for Jung. I think that it is important to realize that his symbols may not be yours. This is also a good book about the use of a journal.

Garfield, Patricia. *Creative Dreaming.* New York: Simon and Schuster, 1975. This is a tremendous book for learning how various cultures approach dreaming, and for realizing that we can change, control, and ask for guidance from our dreams. This would not be a good book for an introduction to the field.

Kelsey, Morton T. *Dreams: Dark Speech of the Spirit.* Minneapolis, Minn.: Augsburg, 1968; paperback ed. *God, Dreams, and Revelation,* 1974. Kelsey has written an incredible sourcebook of the dreams found in the Bible and throughout church history. Kelsey takes the Jungian approach and uses it to support his view that attention to dreams is an integral aspect of the Christian tradition. Little guidance is given for understanding your own dreams.

Perls, Frederick S. *Gestalt Therapy Verbatim.* Moab, Utah: Real People Press, 1969. This includes verbatims of many dreams which are acted out in gestalt fashion. Reading this book is the best way to experience a gestalt approach to dreams, if you do not want to go to a workshop! In this approach, the dreamer is considered to be all parts of the dream.

Sanford, John A. *Dreams: God's Forgotten Language.* Philadelphia and New York: J. B. Lippincott, 1968. Sanford is an Episcopal clergyperson who is now a Jungian analyst. He offers a Jungian perspective on dreams yet is self-conscious of his Christian identity and his pastoral commitments.

Tart, Charles T. *Altered States of Consciousness.* New York: Anchor Books, Doubleday and Co., Inc., 1969. This offers much detailed information about the actual states of dreaming, hypnosis, meditation, and the state between waking and sleeping.

MEDITATION, PRAYER, AND RELAXATION

Benson, Herbert. *The Relaxation Response*. New York: William Morrow and Co., Inc., 1975. This short (125 pp.) book offers a medical understanding of hypertension, a short history of meditation, and a simple technique for meditation which can be adapted to any religion.

Brother Lawrence. *The Practice and the Presence of God*. New Jersey: Fleming H. Revell Company, 1976. This book is available in many editions and translations. It is a Christian classic, about a person who was aware of God at all times!

Chang, Garma Chen Chi. *The Practice of Zen*. New York: Harper and Row, 1970. Good explanations.

Cobb, John, Jr. *To Pray or Not to Pray*. Nashville, Tenn.: The Upper Room, 1974. This is a short autobiographical statement of Dr. Cobb's prayer life. It is honest reflection by a well-known process theologian.

Downing, George. *Massage and Meditation*. New York: Random House, Inc. and Berkeley, Calif.: The Bookworks, 1974. This is a collection of meditations for use during massage. In addition, it offers guidelines which can be used alone. This is very simple and well done.

Dunnam, Maxie. *The Workbook of Living Prayer*. Nashville: The Upper Room, 1974. This is a well organized and fairly traditional workbook for church school or adult education classes. Many who have participated in the sequence recommend it highly.

Jacobson, Edmund. *You Must Relax: A Practical Method of Reducing the Strains of Modern Living*. New York: McGraw-Hill Book Co., Inc., 1957. Written by a medical doctor, this book offers information about and methods for relaxation.

Johnston, William. *Silent Music: The Science of Meditation*. New York: Harper and Row, 1974. Excellent! Johnston, himself within the Hebrew-Christian tradition, is very able to understand, value, and communicate the connecting links between Eastern and Western religious meditation practices. His book uniquely values intimacy as a form of meditation.

Johnston, William. *The Still Point: Reflections of Zen and Christian Mysticism.* New York: Harper and Row, 1970. A good comparison.

The Journal of Transpersonal Psychology. Palo Alto, California. This journal often has articles on meditation.

Kapleau, Philip, ed. *The Three Pillars of Zen.* Boston: Beacon Press, 1967. (1965 published in Japan) This remains one of the best explanations of zen meditation—its practice and its teachings.

Kelsey, Morton T. *The Other Side of Silence: A Guide to Christian Meditation.* New York: Paulist/Newman, 1976. Guided imagery meditation is a part of his approach. Very helpful book.

Le Shan, Lawrence. *How to Meditate: A Guide to Self-Discovery.* Boston, Mass.: Little, Brown and Co., 1974. I recommend this book above all others for a simple description of various types of meditation. Le Shan includes comments on "alluring traps in meditation and mysticism."

Mbiti, John S. *The Prayers of African Religion.* London: SPCK, 1975. This book contains numerous examples of African prayers for many purposes. This is a good introduction to the spiritual questing of some African people.

Merton, Thomas. *Contemplative Prayer.* New York: Doubleday, 1971. Much background material on traditional prayer is packed into this classic.

Merton, Thomas. trans. *The Wisdom of the Desert: Sayings from the Desert Fathers of the Fourth Century.* New York: New Directions Books, 1970. I was very moved by these. They are quite a bit like Sufi sayings: little bits of wisdom, "saying" more than is said.

Naranjo, Claudio, and Ornstein, Robert. *On the Psychology of Meditation*. New York: The Viking Press, 1971. This excellent book offers a comprehensive view of types of meditation, with some examples. I recommend it highly.

Ornstein, Robert E. *The Psychology of Consciousness*. San Francisco, Calif.: W. H. Freeman and Co., 1972. Chapters 5, 6, and 7 focus on meditation. The intent of this book is to document the existence of two major modes of consciousness. It fulfills its intent well. He has suggestions for further reading after each chapter.

Rush, Anne Kent. *Getting Clear: Body Work for Women*. New York: Random House, 1973. There are many good exercises, including relaxation exercises, in this book.

Seifert, Harvey, and Seifert, Lois. *Liberation of Life*. Nashville, Tenn.: The Upper Room, 1976. Like Dunnam's *Workbook*, this offers guidelines for use with a small group. Good ideas.

Selye, Hans. *Stress Without Distress*. New York: The New American Library, 1975. This book focuses upon stress from several points of view. Selye is a medical doctor who writes from that perspective, yet he includes areas such as motivation and values.

Suzuki, Shunryu. *Zen Mind, Beginner's Mind*. Trudy Dixon, ed. New York and Tokyo: Weatherhill, 1970. This is a very good way to begin meditation. Although it obviously offers ideas on the practice of zen, it is relevant to any type of meditation.

Tart, Charles T., ed. *Transpersonal Psychologies*. New York: Harper and Row, 1975. Wow! Top writers offer views from various perspectives: orthodox Western psychology, the paranormal, Zen Buddhism, Yoga psychology, Gurdjieff, Arica, Sufism, and the Christian Mystical Tradition. Although it is long, it is captivating.

Trungpa, Chogyam. *Meditation in Action*. Berkeley: Shambhala Publications, 1969. Trungpa has established several Buddhist contemplative communities in North America.

From Tibet, he offers a lucid understanding of meditation and the qualities of the meditative life.

Underhill, Evelyn. *Practical Mysticism.* New York: E. P. Dutton and Co., Inc., 1915. (paperback) A classic. She looks at the phenomenon of mysticism and offers an explanation which will enable the reader to begin "practice."

White, John, ed. *What Is Meditation?* New York: Anchor Books, 1974. This offers various people's reflections upon and experiences with meditation, under the headings: "What is Meditation"; "How to Meditate"; and "Difficulties, Dangers, and Promises." It would be helpful in offering some insight into what type of meditation is best for you.

Wink, Walter. *The Bible in Human Transformation: Toward a New Paradigm for Biblical Study.* Philadelphia: Fortress Press, 1973. Wink offers a scholarly theological and biblical justification for the experiential study of the Bible. This is a short but challenging book.

INDEX I

Titles of Meditations

The numbers refer to the meditation number, not page number.

INDEX II

Biblical Passages

The numbers refer to the meditation number, not page number.

INDEX III

Suggestions for Use in Daily Life

The numbers refer to the meditation number, not page number.

OCCASIONS

Closing prayer at a meeting or in a group (best if there is time for some debriefing): especially 30; also 5, 7, 8, 11, 12

Crisis: especially 4, 6, 11, 16, 26, 29, 30; also 1, 2, 3, 7, 8, 9, 12, 13, 15, 17, 18, 19, 22, 23, 24, 28

Evening meditation: especially 20; also 2, 4, 6, 7, 8, 10, 14, 15, 18, 22, 23, 24, 26, 27

Morning meditation: especially 25; also 1, 3, 6, 9, 10, 11, 13, 14, 17, 18, 19, 21, 23, 24, 27, 28

Opening prayer at a meeting or in a group: 1, 2, 3, 5, 7

Table grace: especially 21; also 3, 7, 10, 12 (shortened), 14, 23, 25

Vacation: especially 11 and 25; also 1, 3, 4, 5, 7, 8, 9, 12, 13, 14, 17, 18, 19, 21, 22, 23, 24, 26, 27, 28, 29, 30

GROUPINGS

Alone: All except 30 would be appropriate. The following might be especially meaningful: 6, 16, 19, 20, 23, 27, 29

Family: All would be fine. The following would be especially good: 2, 7, 10, 12, 14, 15, 20, 21, 23, 29, 30

Large group: All except 16 would be suitable. In all large groups, attention to debriefing or grounding is important. The following would be especially good for large groups: 2, 9, 12, 21, 25, and 30

Small group: All would be appropriate. The following could be especially meaningful in a small group: 2, 4, 7, 12, 26, 30

With a friend: All would be appropriate. The following would be especially significant for friends together: 2, 4, 7, 12, 14, 15, 23, 26, 27, 29, 30

Note: These suggestions are highly subjective and dependent upon the situation. They are simply my ideas.

INDEX IV

Suggestions for Use in Worship

The numbers refer to the meditation number, not page number.

ORDER OF WORSHIP

Call to Worship: 1, 7, 8, 12, 14, 19, 27, 28
Invocation: 3, 5, 8, 9, 11, 14, 17, 23, 25, 28
Prayer of Confession: 16
Words of Assurance or Forgiveness: 3, 9, 11, 12, 17, 28
Prayer of Confession *and* Words of Assurance, combined: especially 4, 20, and 26; also 2, 3, 5, 7, 8, 13, 14, 15, 18, 21, 22, 24, 27
Affirmation of Faith: 1, 4, 5, 14, 17, 18, 22, 23, 24, 25, 27, 28
Prayer of Thanksgiving: 1, 12, 22, 23, 28
Prayer of Petition and Intercession: 2, 3, 4, 5, 6, 7, 8, 9, 10, 11, 16, 17, 19, 21, 22, 23, 24, 25, 26
Sermon: All would be appropriate within a sermon. Number 30 would require very special circumstances.
Offertory: especially 7; also 3, 5, 9, 12, 19, 21, 24, 25, 27, 28
Communion, Eucharist: especially 15; also 1, 2, 3, 4, 5, 7, 9, 12, 14, 18, 21, 23, 24, 25, 26, 27, 28
Benediction: especially 30; also 2, 9, 11, 12, 19, 24, 25, 27 (encourage "debriefing" later)

SPECIAL WORSHIP SETTINGS

Baptism: 9, 11, 12, 13, 17, 28
Christmas: especially 28; also 3, 9, 14, 17, 27
Concern for the world: especially 5, 18, 21, 25; also 2, 3, 4, 7, 8, 9, 11, 12, 14, 22, 23, 24, 27, 28
Confirmation: 1, 2, 5, 9, 12, 14, 17, 19, 24, 28
Dedication of a building, etc.: 10, 11, 23, 25, 27
Funeral, Memorial Service: 4, 8, 23, 30; maybe 11, 16, 22
Graduation: especially 5, 30; also 1, 2, 4, 9, 11, 12, 15, 17, 19, 24, 25, 27, 28, 29
Ordination: 1, 2, 4, 5, 9, 11, 12, 14, 18, 19, 24, 25, 27
Recognition of teachers, youth, students, etc.: 1, 2, 4, 5, 9, 12, 14, 17, 19, 24
Weddings: 4, 9, 10, 23

INDEX V

Symbols

The numbers refer to the meditation number.